Home

Keeps

Moving

A Glimpse into the Extraordinary Life of a Third Culture Kid

---

by

Heidi Sand-Hart

Home Keeps Moving

This book contains excerpts from Chapter 21 of *To The Ends of the Earth* (Kristian and Ritva Sand, Ooty, Lighthouse Enterprises Pvt. Ltd, 2001).

Written on location in: Ooty and Kovalam Beach [India], Kuksoo [Finland], and London [UK].

Cover photography: Marine Drive, Mumbai (India), 2008 by Heidi Sand-Hart.

McDougal Publishing is a ministry of The McDougal Foundation, Inc., a Maryland nonprofit corporation dedicated to spreading the Gospel of the Lord Jesus Christ to as many people as possible in the shortest time possible.

Published by:
McDougal Publishing
P.O. Box 3595
Hagerstown, MD 21742-3595
www.mcdougalpublishing.com

ISBN 978-1-58158-171-3

Printed in New Delhi, India
For Worldwide Distribution

Dedication

This book is dedicated to all the Third Culture Kids
of this world. Be strong and be true to yourself!

Acknowledgments

To my parents, who gave me the most colourful of childhoods. If given the chance, I wouldn't change anything about it. Thanks for always being there. I love you.

To Samuel and Ben, the best brothers a girl could have! Ben, thanks for being my best friend over the years and understanding the sides of me that hardly anyone does. I wouldn't have wanted to share this insane childhood with anyone else!

To my dear husband Paul, who understands me better than most TCKs! Thanks for your patience and encouragement while I was on this journey, for always believing in me and your wise advice on this book. You're the best life-partner I could've dreamed of. I love you.

To the Leatherbarrow family, who gave me the needed push when I was lacking motivation. Thanks for being my second family.

To all my contributors, who add colour, variety and spice to this book: Andrea Armstrong, Ann Sung-an Lee, Ben Gilbert, Ben Sand, Debbie Ross, Lorena Smith, Jonny Nease and Stephen Weston.

To David Pollock and Ruth E. Van Reken for kickstarting my own TCK processing and inspiring me to write a book of my own.

To Diane and McDougal publishing.

Contents

You Might Be a Third Culture Kid if ...

- You can't answer the question "Where are you from?".
- You speak two languages but can't spell either.
- You flew before you could walk.
- You have a passport, but no driver's license.
- Your life story uses the phrase "Then we went to..." five times.
- *National Geographic* makes you homesick.
- You don't know where home is.
- You realize that furlough is not a vacation.
- You'd rather never say hello than have to say goodbye.
- You read the international section of the newspaper before the comics.
- You have friends in or from twenty-nine different countries.
- You wince when people mispronounce foreign words.
- You never take anything for granted.
- You speak with authority on the subject of airline travel.
- You know how to pack.

- You feel odd being in the ethnic majority.
- You feel you need to move after you've lived in the same place for a month.
- Your pocket money makes you a millionaire in one country and a pauper in the next. [*]
- You've had more vaccinations in your lifetime that you're neighbour's dog back home.
- You consider any travel under eight hours to be a "short trip".
- You are an expert on jet-lag remedies.
- Your few belongings are scattered across three continents.
- You have frequent flyer miles on five different airlines, but not enough on any of them to get a free flight. [*]
- You can easily guess a stranger's nationality by their accent. [1]

If you identify with this amusing and honest list, you might just be a Third Culture Kid! We are indeed a strange, but growing breed since the world is becoming smaller and more cross-cultural. — *HSH*

Foreword by Lorena Smith

I grew up much like Heidi, hovering between several cultures, travelling often, struggling with faith and questions of identity, home, and belonging. My mother is Swedish, my Dad Sri Lankan, and my schooling was all over the place, partly at Hebron School in India, partly in Sweden, partly in the US. To complicate matters more, I married a TCK from Ecuador/El Salvador, with roots in California. We've lived everywhere from Romania to the UK to Connecticut.

As our world grows smaller and smaller, the tribe that is TCK's and ATCK's grow larger and larger. And yet the questions still remain for most of us; where do we belong? How do we fit in? In a world where people put cultural identity and national citizenship in the premier place of personal identity, where are we?

As I read Heidi's book, I was so struck by the way in which I identified and recognized myself in her descriptions and analysis of TCK's. Her story, in some measure, is the story of every TCK, whether missionary kid, or army brat, or diplomat kid, or anyone else.

If you are a TCK, you will recognize yourself and, as I did, breathe a sigh of relief that your experiences and feelings are, after all, universal. If you are a parent, please read this book so you can know what we are and will be going through. And if you are anyone else, those who love us, our friends or coworkers, please read it, because it expresses things we are often hard pressed to put into words.

On the whole, the lives we live, the places we go, and the things we see teach us that people are people everywhere. As you read this book, one of my dearest hopes is not only that you will understand this tribe we call TCK's but that you will also decide to experience what we have—new cultures, new homes, and new people and discover our world.

We will probably run into you somewhere along the way, in Lebanon, Latvia, or London. Come say hello.

Foreword by Ruth E. Van Reken

In today's globalizing world, life is becoming more culturally complex for countless individuals who, for many different reasons, are now growing, or have grown up, among many cultural environments. Rather than living in the world most children in past generations knew–a world where most folks they interacted with operated with the same shared basic set of cultural rules, traditions, and lenses, through which they saw the world–many young people in today's world grow up daily interacting in significant ways with people of widely divergent cultural norms, traditions, and world views. The truth is, as a global community, we are living out a great social experiment on a level never done before. If we learn our personal and cultural identities by having it mirrored back from our surrounding culture, how will this cultural juggling affect the lives of children who grow up among the many worlds rather than just one? No one knows for sure.

But there is one experience from the past that can give us clues for the present and future. In 1984, Dr.

Ted Ward, a sociologist at Michigan State University, declared that third culture kids (TCKs)–those children who were growing up in a culture outside their parents' passport culture for a significant period of their developmental years–were the prototype citizen of the future. He meant that because of changes due to transportation, communication, and trade, children of many backgrounds all over the world, would soon be growing up interacting with many cultural environments and high mobility. When Dr. Ruth Useem named them in the 1950's, TCKs were primarily children of those who had gone overseas for their careers–military, embassy, colonial powers, corporate, and missions.

The major influx of children into these ranks occurred after WWII, when many more people began to settle temporarily overseas because of the increase in multinational companies and trade, coupled with new ease of transportation. If we take a look at the impact of a globally mobile childhood on a child who grows up in that internationally mobile environment, we can examine the longer term impact of trying to learn personal and cultural identity when the mirror around is always changing its message to tell children who they are. Sometimes the local cultural mirror reflects that children are clear foreigners, neither physically resembling the dominant culture nor sharing the traditions or beliefs and values held in the deeper part of that surrounding culture. Other times, however, they may be "hidden immigrants" —physically resembling those around them, but not sharing knowledge of how life in this local culture works. And so it goes.

By looking at TCKs—this community of those who have already lived among many cultural worlds in their formative years—we can also begin to have clues for the possible responses other children may have when they move between cultures for reasons other than their parents' careers. In applying lessons learned from the TCK experience, we can begin to recognize gifts in these other experiences as well. They may be children of minorities who successfully navigate between different cultural environments daily as they go to school in the dominant culture and "repatriate" to their home's culture each evening. Others may be children of immigrants who annually travel back and forth between the parents' former homeland and the new country in which they live to visit grandma. Some are children of bicultural marriages who begin life already negotiating cultural worlds within the walls of their home.

In *Home Keeps Moving*, Heidi Sand-Hart is giving us the opportunity to understand the traditional TCK experience that she and others have known. It is important for us to understand the basic story of those who, like her, grew up internationally mobile for their sake and also for the sake of those who love and work with them. But Heidi's story and those she includes from other TCKs also takes us into the expanding cultural complexity so many face in our world. Heidi is not only a traditional TCK, but she has an added layer of cultural nuances because her parents come from two different countries and cultures. In addition, she did not simply live between one home and one host country but moved multiple times among many. Her story reflects an increasingly common one, where the layering of cultural mixing almost defies comprehension, when compared with a traditional childhood of the past. As you read, you will enter into a better understanding of what many TCKs and other cross-cultural kids (CCKs) experience as they grow up in this "new normal" of increasing cultural complexity.

However, hopefully as you read, you will be able to have deeper insight into your own life story and/ or others you know. Why? Because essentially the TCK story is not about people who are different, but about an experience which may be different from the common ways children grew up in the past. In the end, it is a story of human beings who, like all people throughout the ages, experience joy when they increase their knowledge and awareness of the world, but also experience grief when they lose something they love—be it friend, place, or a stage in life. Like children of all backgrounds, TCKs are shaped by the events and patterns of their formative years. You will learn what some of those common events and responses often are. But, in the end, you will also see that TCKs share the human feelings of joy, pain, celebration, despair, loneliness, belonging, loss, and great gain with others whose stories are quite unlike their own. The context of the stories you will read here is specific. The application of lessons learned from these TCK stories is universal. May you enjoy what you read and grow in the life you live because of what you encounter in the following pages!

Ruth E. Van Reken
Co-author, Third Culture Kids: Growing Up Among Worlds,
Co-founder, Families in Global Transition conference.

Introduction

In this global and transient age, it seems more important to have literature out there for people to grasp and empathise with Third Cultures Kids (TCKs), since cross-cultural living is becoming more common day by day. This is the story of growing up in many worlds.

I wish not nor attempt to speak on behalf of the millions of Third Culture Kids out there. These are simply my perspectives and experiences, and I take full ownership of them. I have made every effort to accurately name dates, places, and references, but with my jumbled upbringing, forgive me the odd mistake.

It is my hope that you gain a wider understanding of the misunderstood race of TCKs, and I have done my best to deliver that opportunity to you. My goal is to bring validation to fellow TCKs—something for them to relate to and empathise with—and insight to help others understand us. Some friends have helped me bring a broader canvas of countries and cultures through their own stories, yet the thread that ties us together irrevocably is simply being TCKs.

This is my story of evolving from a Third Culture Kid into an Adult Third Culture Kid (ATCK), a process that was somewhat delayed, due to the immense pressures of being the child of missionaries. I left home at age eighteen but flew straight into the cocoon of the extended missions family, and was only really able to become my own person in my early twenties.

It was only when I sat down to write this book that I realised what a mammoth task lay before me. I started this project in 2001 (after obtaining a copy of *Third Culture Kids—Growing Up Among Worlds*) and hit a brick wall shortly after. It was mentally too demanding, isolating, and overwhelming at the time, and I found myself drowning in a lack of direction. I abandoned it almost entirely, although my mind returned to it frequently with a growing urgency.

Inspiration returned in the summer of 2009 and the opportunity to pick the project up again. In all honesty, it has been a struggle at times to make progress and sustain any sort of motivation. The subject is so broad, there is much to say, many angles to take, and without other TCKs around to bounce ideas off of, it has been one long, isolating journey. But with encouragement from those close to me and a renewed vigour to make this book a reality, I got there in the end. Now my only hope is that it falls into the right hands.

Heidi Sand-Hart

Chapter One

Introducing Third Culture Kids
(and what is "normal" to them)

The "Third Culture Kid" blanket is large and varied between those with a business, diplomat, army, or religious upbringing. I just happen to fall into the missionary kid bracket, therefore my account is from this perspective.

Nothing about my life and upbringing was "normal". I do not come from one country, but four. Ever since I was born, we have been on the move. I haven't lived in the same house for more than four years, I have been to around nine different schools, lived on three continents, and been to more than forty-two countries (and counting). For the majority of my life, my belongings have been scattered in boxes across three different continents, only to be rediscovered every few years. I have lived in well over thirty different houses thus far and shudder to think how many different beds I've slept in. My definition of "normal" strays about as far from the conventional mold as it possibly could. I had a highly unusual childhood with hints of normality blended in.

Born into the world to a Finnish mother and Norwegian father, I guess you could say I was already dealing with three very different cultures from birth. My parents met while working with the Asian community in London. They were trying to hold onto their Scandinavian culture and traditions and yet allow my brothers and me to immerse ourselves in our country of birth, England. The only real "English" experience we had was at the multiple schools we attended and with some of our friends.

We didn't have the English traditions that my school friends did. We opened our Christmas presents on Christmas Eve instead of Christmas Day, didn't attend football games with our father, and probably had fish and chips monthly instead of weekly. My parents' work targeted the Indian community of England, so we grew up on curry and *chapattis* and were predominantly surrounded by Indians.

There is a term for what I am: "Third Culture Kid" (TCK). This label helps to describe what we are and the reasons behind why we are this way, but the amount of interest in learning about us is not very great, leaving a lot of people out there to misunderstand and alienate us. I am also a "Missionary Kid" (MK), but that part is slightly more straightforward (we accompanied our parents around the world as they fulfilled their God-given calling).

> *"A Third Culture Kid (TCK) is a person who has spent a significant part of his or her developmental years outside of the parents' culture. The TCK builds a relationship to all of the cultures, while not having full ownership of any. Although elements from each culture are assimilated into the TCK's life experience, the sense of belonging is in relationship to others of similar background."* [1]

I remember the first time I heard the phrase "Third Culture Kid". I was seventeen years old, living in India with my parents, and saw an article lying on the coffee table. I picked it up out of interest, and a light bulb went off in my head. I think that was the first time I realised just how different I was, as a result of my unique upbringing and the fact that I was part of a community of global nomads. As a child, you learn to adapt to whatever is thrown at you. It becomes your concept of "normal", and I guess it was too early for me to process the enormity of my whirlwind life.

What Makes Us Different from Adults Who Travel?

"Two circumstances are key to becoming a Third Culture Kid: growing up in a truly cross-cultural world, and high mobility. By the former, Pollock and van Reken mean that instead of observing cultures, Third Culture Kids actually live in different cultural worlds. By mobility, they mean mobility of both the Third Culture Kid and others in their surrounding. The interplay between the two is what gives rise to common personal characteristics, benefits, and challenges. TCKs are distinguished from other immigrants by the fact that TCKs do not expect to settle down permanently in the places where they live.

"Third Culture Kids grow up in a genuinely cross-cultural world. Third Culture Kids have incorporated different cultures on the deepest level, as to have several cultures incorporated into their thought processes. This means that Third Culture Kids not only have deep cultural access to at least two cultures, their thought processes are truly multicultural. That, in turn, influences how Third Culture Kids relate *to the world around them, and makes Third Culture Kids' thought processes different even from members of cultures they have deep-level access to. Third Culture Kids are often tolerant cultural chameleons who can choose to what degree they wish to display their background."* [2]

"The moving back and forth from one culture to another happens before TCKs have completed the critical developmental task of forming sense of their own personal or cultural identity." [3]

Therefore the surrounding cultures had far more of an impact on our young brains and molded their way into our thought processes and lives. Although still an outsider, we saw ourselves as one of them, not superior, different, or away from our "homelands".

The confusion of my multicultural upbringing proved a little too great for my young mind at times, and once, as a two year old, I was surrounded by a group of people speaking Gujarati (an Indian language), I said to my dad: "I don't understand; they're speaking Wegian (Norwegian)"!

I have read various articles written by Third Culture Kids (scarce as they are to find), and the thing that resonates most is how extreme my particular upbringing was. We were catapulted from continent to continent invariably every one to two years. Europe to Asia, Asia to Scandinavia, and back again, adapting so quickly and naturally it would be missed in the blink of an eye. We didn't just face cultural transitions from county to county or state to state, but also continent to continent, constantly shifting between cultures. It is quite remarkable that my sanity lies intact and no wonder that the itch to travel and surround myself with new and different cultures courses through my veins every day.

Chapter Two

Confused Loyalties

> *"A Third Culture Kid is an individual who grows up in a culture other than his own and has a sense of relationship to both or all cultures. He takes pieces of these and has a sense of identity with each of them, but doesn't have a sense of ownership in any of them. The product is what we've come to call the 'Third Culture Kid'".* [1]

I often try to explain my weird relationship to the countries I'm from, but they, too, vary with time. Nothing is simple in my world, and the varying degrees of affection for the nations of my life can often cause confusion or offense.

England is my place of birth and the country in this world that I have spent the most time in. I often get asked which country feels like home to me, and I guess England is that place. I grew up in the streets, fields, forests, schools, parks, football pitches, churches, and shops of England, and much of it is still planted within me. I understand the people, the humour better than anywhere else, and the way things work, which brings me comfort in life. Whenever I arrive in London, the familiarity makes me feel at home...like I almost belong there.

Norway is one of the most beautiful countries in the world. With mountains, glaciers, fjords, beaches, lakes, rivers...it is a natural paradise, and the population of four and a half million keeps it spotlessly clean. Most of my father's family live there, and I have many fond memories of spending time with them. It was never more than a summer holiday destination to me, until we moved there in 1996, and it highlighted a lot of TCK tendencies to me, so for that I am grateful.

Finland is my mother's nation and, sadly, a country that I am still getting acquainted with. I have been to Finland a handful of times, and the older I become, the more I identify with certain aspects of the culture. Finland is called "the Land of a Thousand lakes," and I have pleasant memories of steaming hot saunas, night swims, roasting sausages on open fires, moonlit boat trips with our cousins, adventure, and beauty.

The bare mention of **India** brings a smile to my face and warmth to my soul. It is one of the most captivating nations on earth, and it enters the bloodstream and continues to call you back. So much of my life has revolved around the Indian culture. Even when living in England, we were immersed, accepted, and surrounded by Asians, and it makes me feel at home. I love the craziness of Indian society, the smiling faces that never fail to greet, the fact that you love it one minute and hate it the next, the astonishing nature and history it holds. It is strange to feel so much part of a culture and yet, by the colour of your skin, be viewed as a *feranghi* (foreigner), an outsider.

> *"Confused loyalties can make TCKs seem unpatriotic and arrogant to their fellow citizens."* [2]

I think this is true of many TCKs, but I know I have taken bits and pieces from the different cultures and made them my own. It can be a bonus, since you can choose the things you like about a certain culture and leave out the bad parts. It complicates and makes it harder for people to understand me, since I'm an amalgamation of different world views.

One of the challenges that I have faced within my own family is that we have all adopted different relationships to our various countries. There is not just one country that we all feel completely a part of and that unites us, so there are huge divides when it comes to sporting events. Despite this being a slightly superficial example, it has been hard for each of us, at different times, when other family members don't respond kindly to our nation of choice.

For my father, it has been relatively simple. He is Norwegian. He grew up there uninterruptedly for his entire childhood and into his early adult life. He supports Norway in all kinds of sports and has more clear-cut national pride than the rest of us can muster.

It was hard when we lived in Norway and struggled with his culture, even though he didn't feel entirely at home there either. One of the most open-minded people I know, through all the years of living abroad, he has felt a sense of belonging to many countries. But, naturally, his roots with Norway run deep, and it can't have been easy for him, with us criticising, resisting, and struggling with aspects of it.

By the same token, I feel more patriotic towards England (by a small margin) and am willing to defend many weak aspects of that culture without being blind in my patriotism. It has been difficult for me over the years when some of my family members criticised and disliked aspects of England. Even though I understand where they were coming from, just feeling some sort of connection to a place is special enough and worth protecting.

However, I do struggle with overt patriotism. I understand that it is natural to feel proud of where you come from, but I don't cope well with a raging current of national pride. Anger rises up within me, and I can't explain why, but I find it quite offensive and hard to handle. Those who think theirs is the best country in the world, those who criticise every-thing about other countries when they travel, those who discount the remote possibility that there could be other places out there worth living in ... they make me want to scream and run for the hills! I think its the one-sidedness. I will never know what that feels like, because I have four countries that I am proud of to varying degrees and in different ways. I appreciate that this might be hard for most to understand, but growing up in many worlds complicates the most basic of things.

Through my childhood experiences, a real empa-thy has stayed with me for refugees, the odd ones out, and I suppose it is because I have spent much of my life as just that—the new girl in class, the blond-haired in a multitude of black, the brown-eyed in a sea of blue. Accepted to a degree, but never fully in. To most people, these sentiments would come as a surprise because I come across secure and comfortable, but a deeper soul connection I find with very few.

The Dreaded Questions

In the life of a TCK, even the simplest of questions can be met by the deepest sense of dread. **"Where are you from?"** is a very common question passed around socially, but for me there is no simple way to answer it. My reply can range anywhere from a one-word answer to a mini-version of my life story. My mood generally determines my reply, and I often have to discern whether people are really interested in me as a person, or if I am just a subject of their small talk.

It may sound ridiculous, but I often struggle with betraying myself if I tell people I am only from one country. The reason is that none of the countries of my upbringing fully represent who I am. I am definitely a blend of all the countries I am tied to, and I think I have taken certain parts of all the cultures and made them my own—Norwegian, Finnish, English, and even Indian. Therefore I hate to discredit the others and label myself as being from just one of those places. Others may never understand how huge a part this plays on my life, but I always hesitate before answering that question.

If given the full version, the question that usually follows is: **"Where is home to you?"** and that is equally as difficult. You see, I myself am unsure which nation feels most like home. The truthful answer is that home is wherever my family members are. I haven't really been able to form a strong enough attachment with any country to be able to call it "home". The sense of familiarity I receive when I step foot into one of my home nations is a fantastic feeling, which brings comfort and security to some extent, but I am still very much perceived as an outsider in most of them.

Many people blame TCKs for not having roots established in one country, but seeing the nature of our upbringing, it would be stupid to expect any such easy solution. It is not that I am a rootless individual; I just don't have my roots set where most people do. Mine are planted in people, my family and those who have been involved in my life.

My TCK tendencies seem to emerge brighter when I find myself in a smaller country. Limited mindsets and world view not only anger but isolate me, leaving me feeling like a misunderstood alien. I feel claustrophobic in a setting where people have spent their whole lives together in the same town. Everyone has history with each other, and whether there be a slight measure of jealousy, I feel entirely alone. I feel like those sorts of people don't have the capacity to understand me, so they sometimes don't even bother trying.

I suppose a slight pride emerges from within me,

and I can't help but look down upon their "shallow" talk and immature behaviour. I sometimes forget that not everyone has been exposed to the things I have; therefore they shouldn't be expected to have grasped the same knowledge as me.

An interest in a broad variety of conversation was birthed into me at a young age, a deep interest regarding the state of the world and social issues. My eyes have seen things that most people don't wish to speak of on a Friday night at the pub. I guess it boils down to the fact that, to most people, their local area or country is far more interesting to them than the rest of the world, whereas, with me, the world is what excites me, for I have no physical borders. I am always dreaming of being elsewhere, experiencing new surroundings, cultures, climates, and foods. That is when I feel at "home". That is when my soul comes alive.

Contribution from Ben Gilbert (India-United Kingdom)

"One of the first things that hit me when I started to live in the UK for the first time was the ridiculous amount of choice there was in a supermarket. I never imagined there could be so many types of cheese! Five years on, and I still get stuck in the dairy section with a kind of half-confused, half-perplexed look, lost in concentration, while I try to remember the name of the cheese that I bought last time.

"At first I loved to be different, and I was always the one to

get my upbringing into any conversation. I liked the attention that it got...and the reactions, like, 'Wow! That must have been amazing!' or 'No way! Are you, like, an Indian then?' I found people's naïve perceptions fun to deal with and didn't mind the fact that conversations revolved around the subject of me, me, me!

"When people asked where I was from, I would rush into a detailed description of my parents' work in India, the international boarding school I went to, and how I had only just come to the UK...blaa di blaa blaa blaa. Looking back on that period now, I realise how narrow-minded my thinking was. I had a massive ego, which grew bigger day by day, as I compared my 'exciting' background to what I thought as dull, boring, and mundane 'English' people, who had never really done any 'proper travelling'.

"But this was short-lived. After my initial 6 months of returning to the UK, I started to grow tired of always having to explain my difference in background and inwardly got annoyed with people's joking comments like, 'Ben, this isn't India; we do things like this over here'.

"By the time I got to University, a year after returning to the UK, I started to answer the dreaded question, 'So, where you from then?' with a short, straightforward answer, 'Kent, near Tunbridge Wells', which is true, because that's where I was born! This little trick worked very efficiently, because once I had established myself as a 'normal' English University student, I could be quite selective about how much I would let on about the fact that I was actually not very English at all.

"Of course it didn't always work because my mixed-up accent

would get people guessing where I was from. I got South Africa, Australia, America, Scotland, somewhere 'down south', and then I lost count. Five years on, and I still sound foreign to the English, and English to anyone else. I have asked myself why I sometimes hide my upbringing from people, and I think it is two things: initially it was a need to fit into my 'home culture', and so, in doing so, it was easier to pretend that I was ordinary rather than explaining myself time and time again.

"However, it's obvious that my experience of arriving in the UK has also been shaped by my Christian faith. The whole area of Church/Christian Union/Cell groups (and all the stuff that goes along with that) was another huge adjustment for me. I have to admit that one of the things that I did find hard in University was settling in a church. There was loads of stuff organised for international students and even more on for home students, but neither category really fitted me. Some expected me to become instantly involved in the international group and help with the leadership there, because of all my 'cultural experience'. Little did they realise that I had a heck of a lot of adjusting to do myself, and just because I looked like an Englishman didn't necessarily mean that I thought like one. On the other hand, others expected me just to slot in with the home students and get on with it, which I suppose I did in the end, despite everything. Looking back, I know things would have been better if I'd had the guts just to tell someone exactly how I felt at the time, instead of bottling it up.

"It's always easy to look back in hindsight and think of how I would do things differently. Five years isn't long really, and I still have a fair amount of 'cultural adjustment' to get my head

around, but I hope I have matured in the way that I relate to people close to me and become more sensitive to others, regardless of their background. Somewhere along the line I have a feeling that I've become a little wiser and a little bit more of the person that God wants me to be."

Chapter Three

"Nothing Is Weird, Just Different"

Life was relatively normal during my early years, apart from one detail: my oldest brother Samuel was born mentally handicapped. He lived with us at home when I was younger, but had to move into government care eventually. As a child, I didn't really notice his condition. He was simply a loving older brother who got into trouble a lot! Samuel would sometimes have outbursts, throwing whatever he could get his hands on, but he was never violent with us.

My dad took on most of the 5 AM morning duties of keeping Samuel entertained and knew how to handle him the best. Samuel was very mischievous and would often kick our football into a pond, take a stranger's drink in a restaurant, or throw his shoe out of the car window as we drove on the motorway...and then just laugh hilariously. His laugh could get him off the hook with almost anyone! The doctors thought multiple languages in the home would be confusing for Samuel, so English became our family language, hence my Norwegian suffered.

When I was five years old Samuel moved into government care and while living in England, we would often spend time with him. He had proved too much for my parents, with his constant demands; they had no energy left for us at the end of the day, or anything else, for that matter. They were also feeling more strongly pulled towards India and knew that Samuel would not be able to come along with us on any international trips.

Over the years, Sam became a more distant brother to us, but was always on our minds and in our hearts. We continue to visit him whenever the opportunity arises and stay in touch regularly.

The tables turned on our semi-normal life, and I was five years old, as I boarded my first flight to India. We had packed up our English lives, said our farewells, and were heading into the unknown. Sleep wouldn't come the night before our big journey, for the nerves and excitement were manifesting, as butterflies in my stomach. The night didn't drag on too long, as the alarm clock pierced the darkness at 4 AM, and we hurriedly brushed our teeth and bundled into the car.

The Kuwait Airways flight took off, and we could barely contain our excitement. It was our first long-haul flight, and the stewardesses took extra special care of us, even allowing us a visit to the cockpit. The stop-over in Kuwait felt like days, as jetlag blurred with new impressions: spotless marble floors, ladies covered with *abaya* (black over-garments), men wearing white shirts that went to their ankles (*dish dasha*), prayer rooms in the airport. It was an entirely foreign world.

The minute we stepped off the plane, I knew India was going to be nothing like the quiet, orderly home I'd left behind! At "Smelly Delhi" airport, instead of a customs desk, there was simply a sign that read "Health Check", with no other explanation. People were pushing in everywhere, and it appeared to be utter chaos. After fighting our way through what turned out to be immigration, we proceeded to baggage claim, only to find a gigantic heap of suitcases thrown hastily in the middle of the room! In 1986, this was India's system for reclaiming luggage. My dad had to climb the mountain of bags, clambering his way through, to find our suitcases!

Some people don't even last a full day in India before running for the first flight home, and I could see why, as culture shock hit instantly. The humidity and strange smells stood out, then the crowd of people pushing to get to us first: "Taxi? You want taxi? Rickshaw? Money change? Hotel, sir?…" Beggars slept wherever they could find a spare inch, and there were seas of people everywhere. Tiredness and shock overwhelmed me, as every Indian standing tried to take advantage of the "fresh off the plane" foreigners.

It took a few days to get used to our new surroundings…the noise, smells, dirt, crowds, spicy food, chaos, traffic, poverty, smiles…but soon enough we found ourselves captivated and fascinated by India. Although we were quite used to Indian food from England, the bacteria was altogether foreign, and it didn't take long before I had my first upset tummy. They put chillies in everything (even Western food), and it was hard to get adjusted to such hot food.

Being cute little blond kids earned us far more attention than expected and had its benefits. It appeared we could get away with anything, as the locals picked their noses in public, spat everywhere, burped in the finest of restaurants, and relieved themselves wheresoever they pleased. It was a weird contrast, coming from a land of politeness and queues, to the apparent disorder of India.

For someone who prefers the back row, this instant celebrity took a little getting used to. I hated how the locals would stare at me for hours on end. It didn't matter whether you were on a train, bus, or in a restaurant, their fascination was uncontrollable, and I found it rude and annoying initially. People would touch our hair or pinch and twist our cheeks (really hard) in wonder, but it wasn't entirely harmless. Ben and I soon developed big white marks on our cheeks, as a result of all the touching from dirty hands. We had to get a special infection cream from Norway to clear it up. The clearly defined personal-space bubbles of England that I was used to didn't apply here. Ben and I attempted to copy the head gestures the Indians used and marvelled at how shaking from side to side meant "yes" instead of "no". Everything and anything was carried on the heads of the people, and we were in awe of all these wonderful surprises. People were so friendly and helpful; they often cycled miles just to get us soft drinks and treats.

As we travelled around North India, we saw dire living conditions and poverty which made the sacrifices we'd made seem quite insignificant. It brought a new appreciation for all we had and often took for granted in the Western world. I remember one incident in India that will stay with me forever:

I was six years old at the time, and Ben was nine. We were in Uttar Pradesh, visiting some friends, who took us to a Sunday school meeting for poor children. We learnt that none of the children in the meeting had bowls or plates to eat from, and this really affected us. Before we left England, Ben and I had decided to save up our pocket money and take it to India to give to some poor people. We saw that this was the perfect opportunity, so we went to the market with my mum and bought eighty to one hundred new plates and gave them out to these poor children at the next meeting. We were happy to help in a practical way, despite our own young age, and I guess a desire was born within me.

India seemed like one big adventure playground, and somewhere that we fit into quite naturally. The life, colour, and vibrancy were addictive, and there was always something going on: nonstop action.

Squat Toilets and Bucket Baths

A year later, in 1987, India was to become our new home. We made our way to South India for the first time, to a former British hill-station called Udaga-mandalam (Ooty). Known as "the Switzerland of India", it sits two thousand, two hundred metres above sea level, among the Nilgiri Hills, and re-quires a three- to four-hour bus ride from the plains to reach. The ascent takes you through palm tree forests, lush winding hills, tea plantations, beauti-ful waterfalls, crumbling red earth, tropical flowers, monkeys playing by the roadside…the most memo-rable and nerve-wracking journey of my childhood.

We climbed the Nilgiris in a rickety old bus, filled to the brim with locals. Croaking around the thirty-six hair-pin bends, the bus struggled to navigate the sharp turns, and more than once we came close to disappearing over the edge.

My dad had come out earlier in the year to sort out schooling and housing for us, so all we had to do was settle in. Montauban Guest House became our Indian home. It was beautiful and serene, with plenty of space outdoors to play and be adventurous. I was thrilled to have so much space and friends to roam the landscape with.

The school term had already started, so Ben and I were admitted into Hebron School. I had the usual first-day nerves, but they dissipated soon with the warm welcome I felt. There was a distinct family atmosphere within the rich blend of different cultures. Hebron was a boarding school primarily for missionary and business children, so we had students and teachers from all over India and the world. We were thrilled with the facilities, which included a swimming pool, tennis court, football pitch, cricket ground, and indoor sports hall. The surrounding nature was beautiful, and Hebron was safely tucked away on a hill, with eucalyptus forests hiding it away from the madness of India. The education level was far higher than England, so we had to work really hard in the beginning to catch up.

My parents decided to live in Ooty so that we didn't have to board at school where children as young as five years old lived in separate boys and girls dormitories and only saw their parents on holidays. This sacrifice was felt mostly by my mum, since she couldn't accompany my dad on his various missionary trips around India, but it was a sacrifice she was happy to make and one that I am most grateful for.

Instead of the usual class trips to the zoo, we visited tiger and elephant inhabited jungles, crystal clear lakes, and neighbouring hill stations. Coming from the concrete jungle of London, the variety was incredible. Weekly "clubs" included sailing, rock-climbing, kayaking, and a whole variety of crafts and sports. School life was rich in so many ways, and we learnt lots about different cultures from our fellow students.

One time when my dad was away, we heard loud thuds on the roof of our flat. We were scared that someone was trying to break in. The Montauban watchman rushed to our aid, but, to everyone's amusement, the perpetrators were a band of monkeys who made a surprise visit from their home halfway up the mountain!

Heavy rains started falling shortly after we arrived and continued on relentlessly for weeks. This was my first taste of Indian monsoon, and the excitement soon dissipated, as the earth turned muddy, and rivers emerged from everywhere. During one monsoon, there was a large landslide on the mountain road between Coimbatore (the nearest large city) and Ooty. News reached us that the cascading earth had tragically pushed a bus and lorry off the cliff and completely destroyed the main road. Transportation from the plains was halted for weeks and, with it, food supplies from around India could not be imported to Ooty. We ran out of daily necessities like butter and bread for a little while, and it was the talk of the town.

We learned that it was a Hebron tradition to go to Kovalam beach (in Kerala) for the autumn half-term break, so we set off on the night train with newly-formed school friends and parents in tow. We reached the shores of Lighthouse Beach just as the sun was rising and couldn't contain our excitement. Shoes came off, and we waded in the tropical warm waters surrounded by palm trees. It truly felt like paradise. A few shacks lined the beach, serving as restaurants and hotels, and, within no time, we felt welcomed by its warm embrace. Such paradise holidays had never been afforded us in England, and we swam for hours upon end, until we were red and sunburned.

Over the years, I have seen the changes brought on by charter flights and global tourism, but Kovalam

Beach remains one of my favourite places to this day. It is one of the few places that I have history built up with the locals, since I was seven years old. The place may change, but the people remain.

As our first Ooty winter drew near, it brought with it a distinct chill (freezing for Indian standards, mild for Europeans), and it was cold enough to warrant using a hot water bottle at night. After the comforts of England, it was quite an adjustment, without central heating, and having a bucket bath on the cold stone floor was difficult at first. Hot water was carried up to our flat from the main boiler room by the kind Montauban staff, and one bucket of water was all we got. Life was simple, without running hot water, television, and reliable power, but that, in itself, had its charm. It was, of course, frustrating when we sat down in the communal lounge for "movie night", and the electricity would go half way through the film! That became the norm, and our candle supply was always abundant. Despite all this, Montauban was the perfect home for us, with the constant flow of guests and buzz of activity.

Soon enough, Christmas was upon us, and only now do I realise how bizarre it was to eat a traditional English Christmas dinner in the mountains of South India! The winter holidays lasted two months, which enabled us to experience much of India and even Bangladesh (on visa runs). My parents combined holiday with seminars and crusades, so we saw many facets of India. It was common for us to spend twenty-four to forty-eight hours on trains, travelling the length and breadth of the country, from the southernmost tip of Kanyakumari to the northwestern deserts of Rajasthan. We learnt a lot about Indians, whilst on those arduous second-class train journeys, and laughed at the delays and chaos. From oceans to deserts, to mountain ranges, we saw plenty, and one of the most breathtaking sights in my life was seeing the sunrise over the Himalayas, not to mention the Taj Mahal. India is a land of immense beauty, and it saddens me to see how often it is portrayed negatively...as nothing more than the slums of Calcutta or Mumbai.

Orphanages and Transitions

Our family continued to ping-pong between England and India, and it seemed our time in India always flew by. Over the course of many travels, it didn't take long to notice that I was a second-class citizen in India compared to Ben, "Master Ben", Ben the BOY. Most people would seek only Ben's opinion, which left me feeling slightly insignificant. I had been hurled into a man's world with no other option but to accept it. Due to Samuel's absence, Ben and I became quite close over the years, and at times it felt like there was just the two of us. Of course, like all siblings, we had our ups and downs, but the one thing we had through all the changes and transitions was each other. Our family life was great. We ate out more often than we could in England and had weekend trips to the local Wildlife Sanctuary, to ride elephants and swim in the rivers.

For as long as I can remember, my mother has had a special place in her heart for children, especially orphans. She was able to bring her dream to reality during the years we lived in Ooty and started two orphanages for girls. Due to the dowry (money, possessions, and property) that girls have to bring to a boy's family in marriage, girls are often unwanted and overlooked in India. Poor people go to disturbing lengths to rid themselves of their unwanted baby daughters. One of our rescued babies had been left in the jungle for the tigers; another was bought to save her from a life of prostitution. I loved having little sisters and spent as much time as I could playing with them and helping out with their care.

Chapter Four

"Swimming in Two Cultural Oceans" [1]
(outside looking in)

"The TCK awareness that there can be more than one way to look at the same things starts early in life." [2]

We experienced reverse culture shock every time we returned to England, which was quite frequently. The cleanliness, quiet, ease, and peaceful order seemed just as foreign to us as the extremes of India. During our years in England, I also felt very much at home, despite moving from home to home, church to church, and school to school.

Parts of East London felt like being back in India (despite the gloomy weather), and we continued to be immersed in curry, colourful clothing, and Indian languages. We had regular visits from Aunty Laura (our adopted English grandma, who had a hand in raising all three of us), Samuel, and other friends and relatives from afar. There was always some Indian preacher or friend passing by, and I loved the action.

My parents started numerous churches for Indians and Pakistanis in and around East London, and one was situated right next to Upton Park (West Ham's football ground). As we played football in the car park, the cheers of match-day hooligans merged with Indian worship songs.

Many of our British-born Indian friends were struggling to relate to the very different cultures they found themselves tied to. They felt, acted, and sounded British in many respects, but were also expected to fall into line with their family's culture, language, and traditions. Some of their parents didn't even speak or understand English, yet the kids were fluent in cockney slang. I saw some of my friends act in completely contradictory ways, depending on whether they were with me or in front of their families. My girlfriends became submissive Indian daughters at home, quiet and subservient, yet outside they were like any other East Londoner on the street. They were torn between the two very different worlds, and one of my friends had to sac-rifice love for the family's choice of marital partner. It seemed that everyone around me was relating to two or more cultures and able to play the appropriate part when called upon. That, to me, seemed normal, since I myself was continually floating between cultures.

Throughout our London years, my parents tried to hold on to their Scandinavian roots quite strongly. We had *pulla* (a traditional Finnish pastry) every Saturday afternoon, and my mum cooked Norwegian, Finnish, Indian, and English food. We went to a few Finnish Christmas parties and had Scandinavian friends and regular saunas at the Finnish Seamen's Mission in London. We were sent Donald Duck comic books in Norwegian from relatives (which is how I learnt to read basic Norwegian) and Finnish sweets. Most summers were spent in Norway, swimming in lakes, and enjoying the safety and freedom that country provided.

We got along really well with our Norwegian cousins (many of which were also TCKs), yet I didn't feel a sense of belonging in Norway and chose to speak English, despite understanding a lot of Norwegian. We also attended "family gatherings" in either Sweden or Finland, where my mum's huge family gathered from various parts of the globe, and got along really well with those cousins too. It was these trips that kept us feeling connected and bonded to our relatives.

Unlike a lot of missionary kids, I wasn't sheltered from the "real world", tucked away in a safe cocoon. East London life exposed me to all kinds of things, and I quickly learnt to keep my head down and be "street smart". Stories and scenes of violence surrounded us, but I never felt too unsafe. Some of the kids at my school were really mean, teasing the poorer and less socially accepted students, and I always felt sorry for the outcasts.

TCKs are often exposed to things at a tender age that many of their friends back home have never been faced with. Seeing drastic poverty, beggars and inhumane living conditions, has the potential to mature us a lot earlier on in life. Being surrounded by older people in our various communities gives us an interest in things beyond our years, such as politics and international relations. Many of us live in parts of the world where tensions run high between ethnic groups, and it becomes everyday life to us, not just something seen on TV.

I may have had difficult transitions for various reasons, but many TCKs live in volatile and dangerous places. The following account is from a friend who was attending Murree Christian School in Pakistan when it was attacked by terrorists.

Contribution from Stephen Weston (UK-Pakistan-Thailand)

"Nearly every morning I would pick up a basketball and take a shot. While the ball was in the air, I said to myself, 'If this goes in, it's going to be a good day'. This Monday morning I missed, by a long way.

"I was sitting in English class, looking over some work that my teacher had handed back, occasionally pulling faces at my friends on the other side of the table. Suddenly, several successive bangs rang out in the damp air. I knew from the beginning that it was gunfire; I just didn't want to believe it; none of us did. In the next few moments, we all got under our desks and began praying. More bangs. I couldn't help thinking of my little brother, somewhere in the school getting shot, or my sick mother and my father up in the hostel building, being murdered by terrorists.

"I heard the huge door of the school building slam closed. I had this feeling deep inside me that they were in the building. At that moment, I crawled as far under the desk as possible. High-pitched screams echoed through the old converted church building. Now I was absolutely sure they were inside.

"After a few minutes, we were told that it would be safe to move into the next-door classroom and join with students there. On my way out of the room, I took a quick glance out the window, which opened into the school hall. I saw what I thought was a dead body, lying in a pool of blood. People were all around this woman, helping her. Maybe she wasn't dead.

"As we all got under our desks in the next-door classroom, we began to pray for the protection and safety of all on the school compound. I even prayed for the terrorists. I don't know why. We also began singing.

"More bangs, although further away now. Being in a top room of the old, cold, walled building, it seemed as though they were still shooting in the same place they had begun.

"After about thirty minutes, which felt like an eternity, a

teacher came and filled us in on the situation. People began to rise cautiously from under their desks. Six people had been killed. They included two security guards, a cook, a carpenter, the receptionist, and an 'innocent' bystander. But they were all innocent, weren't they?

"The receptionist, Baber, was a good friend of mine. I used to play cricket with him. He was a great bowler. It was strange to think that I wouldn't ever play cricket with him again.

"The screams we had heard were those of a few friends. They had seen Mrs. V come in covered in blood. This was the woman that I thought was dead. She had been shot in the arm and had lost a lot of blood. She was on her way to the hospital as we spoke.

"After another half an hour, more shots. Everyone was back on the floor under the desks. Word came that it was a false alarm; one of the army men had fired a shot by mistake. We were then told we could make our way down to the school hall.

"We walked down the stairs to the hall, crouching as low as possible when going past the windows. I was happy to see my brother and mum. I looked around. 'Where was dad?' I thought. Finally I saw him in the far corner, looking after some younger children. I saw some of my friends from another class and went to talk to them.

"After a meeting with the school director, it was lunchtime. The walk up to the dining room was the longest walk ever. I was shaking, I felt sick, and I was numb. As I walked up the last few steps, I saw that a car had been moved to cover up a pool of blood. I saw smashed windows and dents in the concrete walls from the gunfire. The floor was red, and the smell was horrible.

"Lunch was the school cook's attempt at Spanish Rice. It didn't taste good without tomato ketchup. As I squeezed the bottle, it reminded me of what I had seen on the floor outside. I managed to eat some of my lunch, but I was feeling far too ill to finish it.

"After a longer talk with some friends and lots of hugs, I went down to the school again. As I walked, I was conscious of someone watching me. My walk became a slow jog, which, in turn, became a fast run. I went into the student lounge and put on some music. The beats reminded me of the gunfire, so I turned it off.

"I thought someone was there and began to run out of the hall. I didn't feel safe when I was alone. I ran up to my parents' apartment and closed the door behind me. Mum and dad were in; they were watching my brother play on the playstation. I sat down and watched too. The green formula-one car of Jenson Button was roaring around the corners at breakneck speeds. It churned my stomach to watch. I ran into my room, and the door slammed closed. I jumped, for it reminded me of the gunshots.

"I dived under my bed and began praying for God to keep me safe. Mum, dad and Phil came in and tried to comfort me and get me to come out. I said that I didn't want to get shot, so I wasn't coming out. I stayed there for half an hour, crying and crying. I couldn't stop; it just went on and on.

"The minutes passed. I got out from underneath the bed and felt the wet carpet. The door opened, and I fell to the floor and covered my head. Nothing happened. As I looked up, mum came and gave me a hug.

"I went down to the computer lab so that I could email friends and family, but I made sure that I was with someone this time. I felt a lot more secure, having someone with me.

"I went down to the hall again and picked up a ball. With long, wet streaks falling down my face, I looked at the blurred ball and thought to my self, 'That was a bad day'.

"It doesn't really feel that long ago now, but when I think of everything that I've been through since, it could be decades!

"The school closed immediately following the attack. The school board met, and the decision was made to move the high school to Thailand. Within seven weeks, the school was opened, and learning began again, but this time in Chiang Mai.

"Things were different, so different. We'd gone from an Islamic country to a Buddhist one. From a country that had odd, large advertisements for toothpaste and biscuits, to a country where adverts consisted of bikini-clad women with alcohol. While walking in the market, men thrust images of prostitutes in front of you. Such different cultures! Suddenly it wasn't just a mix of Islamic and British; there was a third influence on how I lived my life.

"Moving from Murree to Chiang Mai was difficult, but the move was made a lot easier by the fact that the whole high school was going through it together. This was something that I hadn't got when the year in Thailand finished.

"We got back to England in time for the 'summer'. As it rushed by, I realised that settling down in the UK was difficult. I began college, and that also took a long time to get used to. Rather than life being based on spending time with your friends, playing sport, or talking with others about global situations, it was now based on what happened in Eastenders or Hollyoaks (British soap operas), how drunk you were at the weekend, who your girl/boyfriend was, and how your sex life was. It seemed *to be the only thing that people at college spoke about. All I could think was, 'Are all people my age in England like this?'*

"Church helped me to answer that question. I started going along to the youth group, and finally I felt as though I had been welcomed back to England. But it wasn't just church that helped me adjust. It was time. And it does take time to adjust to things.

"Seven and a half years on, I think I would say that I'm settled. And I might even go so far as to say that England is my home now. But I've still got itchy feet."

In my preteens, I started connecting with and relating to people of all ages. I had lots of friends my own age from school, but I began spending time with people considerably older than me. We always had adults in and out of our house, and I guess we had learned to relate to them with immense ease. I often feel OLD in social settings, not in the physical sense, but because of all the different experiences I've had. My eyes have seen so much of this glorious earth.

As with everything, there are positives and negatives. The positives can allow you to develop a world view and appreciate material possessions more, yet hold on to them less. But it often creates a gap when returning to our friends at home; relating becomes harder and isolation can set in. Without the luxury of growing up with the same people our whole lives and with all the back and forth, we miss chunks of contemporary culture: the new pop bands, TV shows, or gadgets. There are time lines and pieces of knowledge missing from our social catalogue, which can single out and humiliate us at times. Not knowing what is appropriate to wear at a nightclub or a Western wedding, for example. In India, we weren't allowed to dance at school, let alone go to nightclubs, and the only weddings I'd been to were Indian.

I've had my fair share of committing social *faux pas* (for lack of knowing any better) and have been caught out on basic knowledge a few times. I was once asked, by an Englishman, what colour the door of 10 Downing Street was (something, I suppose, that all who claim to be British should know). I answered incorrectly (red, instead of black), and felt slightly stupid. For some reason or another, that particular piece of information fell through the cracks with me. Maybe it wasn't all that important in my global world. These are common occurrences for TCKs, and people sometimes think we are less intelligent than we actually are, due to these simple social blunders. It makes it harder to feel a sense of belonging to a culture, when you have such gaping cultural or historical gaps of knowledge.

I remember returning to England on many occasions and finding my friends stuck on "fickle" things, without having a clue what was happening in the rest of the world. They often failed to show any signs of interest in my exciting Indian adventures, yet I was expected to jump back into their (supposedly shallow) worlds, without a thought or tear. It is natural that you only feel connected with your friends to a certain extent. There is a line of separation from your other life that you carry alone.

You learn that, the world over, people are consumed with their bubbles of life and hardly break outside of them in their way of thinking. This, of course, becomes another thing we cannot relate to, because we have more than one bubble. For some of us, we have many. We have seen that there are many different ways to do the same thing, and all of them have their place. We have acquired the ability to see and understand things from both perspectives, which sets us apart, especially at a young age. This can make it difficult to ever be satisfied with one cultural "bubble".

Contribution from Andrea Armstrong (Canada-Indonesia-Singapore)

"...I can only write about my own personal experiences. One of the biggest challenges for me, as an MK, has been this: in all the moving back and forth that my family has done, it's always been a bit difficult for me to find where I fit in socially, especially in my 'home' country, Canada. I think that the things I experienced were so different from what many others my age in North America have seen, that we couldn't completely relate on the same level. And I was also a little hesitant to share with people what I was all about. I guess I tend to feel a bit protec-

tive about my experiences.... They are a part of my past life
that I hold rather sacred....

"My parents were missionaries in the interior of West Kaliman-
tan, Indonesia. With the exception of two furloughs, when I
was quite young, I lived the first twelve years of my life in a
house surrounded by jungle, two hundred and fifty km from
the nearest city. A river ran behind our house, and an airstrip
stretched out in front.

"My brother, sister, and I were home-schooled each morning by
my mom. We always got schoolwork finished as soon as possible
because we didn't want it to consume our entire day.

"Every afternoon I played with kids from surrounding villages.
We played games that involved some elastic bands, or a stick
and some stones. Sometimes we wandered around in the jungle,
looking for wild vegetables to bring home for supper. We each
carried small machetes for cutting bamboo shoots, and large
baskets on our backs to hold the various ferns, leaves, and shoots
we found. Or maybe I'd join them at their family's rice field, to
help in a day's work of harvesting.

"Sometimes we wandered to the outskirts of the animistic
graveyard and dared each other to go in, meanwhile scaring
each other, telling ghost rumours. And then we'd always end
the day by jumping into the river for our mandi, our bath. This
was usually the highlight of the day for everyone, and there was
less actual bathing accomplished than swimming and playing.

"These were some of the best years of my life....

"My family moved back to Canada just as I was entering junior
high. There, for fun, people watch movies or go out for a meal.
They spend their days in offices and classrooms, bathe under

a shower of clean water, and buy vegetables from the super-market. I don't think that any of these things are bad; they're just so different from what I was used to. I entered a different culture and style of life than I was accustomed to.

"Along with the challenge of adapting to a new culture, sur-roundings, and climate, I also had to face the challenge of finding friends. I was suddenly surrounded by a large majority of middle-class Caucasians who'd lived in the same house, at-tended the same school, and had the same friends their whole lives. Many had never travelled beyond a two-hour radius of their home.

It was difficult for me to share with others who I really was. I certainly didn't want to conform, to be 'normal' like the others, but I also was afraid of opening myself up to the possibility of rejection. So, I think, I hid part of myself from others. I became accepted and liked by students and teachers, but never really opened myself up to deeper relationships.

"I often felt awkward for being different than others, but, at the same time, I didn't actually want to be like everyone else. I wanted distinction. I was the only one in my class who'd lived most of my life in a far-off rainforest. I was the only one who'd seen monkeys in the wild, held a monkey, and eaten monkey... , the only one who had swam in the South China Sea... , the only one who'd seen third-world poverty first-hand... . I quite loved the fact that I was different from everyone else. I wanted distinction, and I wanted to be accepted for that. And I feel the same way even now. A fear of mine is that I'll end up living a 'mediocre' life, stuck in one place for the rest of my earthly existence.

"The more I see of this beautiful world, the more of it I want to see. And I think the downsides of 'social inadeptivity' or other not-so-fun results of having lived as a TCK in no way compare to the exciting opportunities I've had to witness the beauty of God's creativity first-hand. I'm so thankful... ."

The ability to adjust and adapt between different cultures is remarkable but completely natural. Our accent and demeanour can change, depending on where in the world we are. We have been described as cultural chameleons, and sometimes, due to the constant adapting, it can be hard to figure out who we really are. I am completely used to feeling alone in a crowd, even when they are speaking a language that I understand.

Chapter Five

The Unquenchable Search
(for a "home" that doesn't exist)...

"If you came back, you wanted to leave again; if you went away, you longed to come back. Wherever you were, you could hear the call of the homeland, like the note of the herdsman's horn far away in the hills. You had one home out there and one over here, and yet you were an alien in both places. Your true abiding place was the vision of something very far off, and your soul was like the waves, always restless, forever in motion." [1]

"Their emergent lifestyle produces a third culture that lacks national or cultural boundaries. TCKs are marginal, mobile in body, soul, and

intellect. Their roots lie in uprootedness. They
fit in everywhere, nowhere in particular. They
are simultaneously insiders and outsiders." [2]

I believe restlessness is one of the biggest struggles for TCKs and ATCKs alike; this is certainly true for my friends and me. The negative connotation associated with words like *restlessness* and *rootlessness* is unfair to TCKs, and we spend a lot of our lives defending this part of our make-up. The fact that going is as natural to us as staying needs to be taken into consideration. It is all we've known, and therefore it becomes our normality. The fact that much of the world hasn't lived this way doesn't make our experience wrong or negative. Of course there are attributes formed as a result of our lifestyles that aren't too healthy, but this goes for everyone, no matter whether you grew up in a village or out of a suitcase.

Brian Lev, now in his mid-thirties, recalls home as:

"made up of those memories and emotions I have collected over time, from which I draw comfort and strength as needed. In effect, home is the place where I can go in my mind, where culture is a mix from many places, and belonging can be taken for granted. ... It's as if we [global nomads] have replaced the physical home of non-nomads ...with an internal home we can go to when we need a respite from the world. I think of us as looking out at the world from a place inside that we share with other nomads." [3]

I prefer to focus on the many positives of my upbringing that cannot be bought or attained in adulthood. The experiences, knowledge, memories, friends, and places become my roots, my sense of belonging, and my version of home. "Home" doesn't consist of four walls, just as church isn't merely the building. For me, home is found in a variety of places and people. The instrumental people in my life throughout the formative years (who were from many cultures and nations) create a home feeling when I'm with them. Having history with people becomes more important as life spreads you far and wide. I don't have a lot of friends whom I've known since birth, so the ones I do have are worth gold.

But onto the struggles that all this moving brings. I will be the first to admit that, to me, the grass indeed is always greener on the other side. I tend to glorify the future, cling to the past, and have trouble ever actually settling into the present. It's natural to let your mind wander to the vibrant, bold, and warm, when all that surrounds you is grey, dull, and dreary.

I do believe there is an element of romanticising certain countries or seasons of our lives, but this is natural. You know there is more out there. You know you don't have to be confined and accept one way of life, because the world is full of different ones. However, this does make it hard to be content where you are, when things become routine and dull, and I guess there is an unrealistic element about childhood that is hard to attain in adulthood. I struggle to accept that life won't be as exciting and varied as it was growing up. Realising that "real life" is mundane, even unglamorous at times, is a hard pill to swallow. We have been gifted a level of variety and excitement that is hard to re-create and take into adult life. It is dangerous to take into adult life, because then we truly do become isolated from our peers, drifters without a support base.

Whether our roots lie in places or people, I think we all need consistent friends in our lives that have our best interests at heart and can help us through the maze of life. It takes time and commitment to form those bonds, which means sacrificing the free-roaming adventure for a season or two. My concept of "settling down" is staying put somewhere for a year or two. I look upon that as a great achievement, but that, of course, is preposterous to most people.

Contribution from Ben Sand (Norway-Finland-England-India)

"Life for me is the smell of the red earth in Tamil Nadu just after the sweet monsoon rains scatter leaving the eucalyptus trees bent and fragrant. It's the crisp clear air of the Norwegian forests. It's the rattling of the underground going between Bank and Liverpool St station. It's the In and Out Burger neon sign lit up against an LA sky. It's the parks in summer sitting drinking beer in Copenhagen with dear friends. It's the moments of

autumn sat by a canal in Amsterdam alone watching the boats pass. It's a hot bag of fresh samosas from Salman Butt's take-away in Chungking Mansions, Hong Kong. Its the constant rain and foggy windows of a Taipei cab rushing past thousands of scooters. It's the nights spent in Finnish saunas with your family remembering times past and planning the future.

"These are not holiday memories. They are my life. The very threads that create my story. Inseperable. Completely ingrained in my psyche and persona. I long for those moments when stuck in a place I feel uncomfortable in, or when the pull to travel starts tugging at my soul. Although they always seem more rosy in retrospect, I am almost always certain they are better than where I am.

"Life is what you have been exposed to, have understood or have grown up creating. Mine has been one of constant change, of constant sorrow in leaving friends, of constant changes in climate and culture, language and attitudes, I belong nowhere but everywhere. I find a little piece of myself in many places, its impossible to collect them all and plant them any one place, since a tree cannot grow in the desert and likewise a collection of uneven pieces cannot be placed together perfectly. There will be holes. There will be problems, lack.

"Home has never really been an issue for me. I adapt pretty quickly. Home can be somewhere I have lived for only a month or two, or a city I have spent years in. It has also been the couch in a friend's house, a hotel room, a hammock. Home to me has always been the feeling or connection I get when around a select group of people, obviously my family, but also other

TCK's with whom you skip the irritations of explanations and get straight to the meat of the conversations and memories. I guess it stems from the fact that moving so often and to such opposite areas of the world demands you to settle quickly, since you don't know how long you will be there and where you will be heading to next. I think four years is the longest I have lived in a single house, back when I was seven years old. Ever since that time the longest period has been a year or two, the shortest a couple of months. My body has become accustomed to moving, to packing, to sailing, flying, driving, so much that when I stay somewhere for a while I begin to think of where I could go next, or if I could hop over to the neighbouring country for a weekend or something.

"Many people ask me if I am rootless or restless. I guess to an extent that's true, although I have grown up treating continents as cities, countries as streets nearby. To me I have roots in many different places, scattered overseas, but all of them are such a deep part of who I am that I return to them often to visit the places I grew up, the friends I don't get to see that often. My roots are longer than others, perhaps not deeper, but longer since they have to reach all the way to India while I am in Amsterdam, all the way to England when I am in Denmark.

"Almost everywhere I stay I make a valid attempt to interact with the locals, shopkeepers, bartenders, taxi drivers, guards, bus drivers. To try and fit in, learn something new yet maintain a healthy amount of distance (unless you meet real soulmates) so that farewells are not too heartbreaking. The hunger for exploring the world and understanding new things spurs me on. The

thought of settling down with a family, a house, a mortgage, a car, a permanent job is not even a fixture in my thinking. At thirty-two I have already succumbed to the fact that most of my friends are married, half way into careers, owners of their third or fourth car, masters of weekend dinner parties or movie nights with their kids. These are things I can admire but do not aspire to replicate. I want certain things from life which may not come due to the path I have chosen, but we all have to surrender some dreams in exchange for others. I have rarely met people who can successfully balance travelling with a healthy marriage. It is possible. I hope to attempt it at some point in my life. But for now, home is where my friends are, where my memories lay, where the new day breaks over a silent beach. I don't need anything deeper than that, yet."

We are a strange and unique breed who feel more at home in airports than shopping centres. All we have to hold on to are photographs and memories, but even they fade with time. The diversity and colour given to us in our childhood spurs us on to find something similar out of our adult lives. Whether it be seeing the past through rose-coloured glasses or that people are more consumed with playing it safe these days, I don't know, but I struggle to accept that life has to be lived the traditional way. And why should it, when our upbringings have showed us there is always another way?

Contribution from Lorena Smith (Sri Lanka-Sweden-India)

" *'Welcome to London, Heathrow. The temperature is 15 degrees Celsius and there is a light rain. . . . ' I smile. I have never ever touched down in London when there wasn't a light rain. I love that first time you step outside the halls of the airport and breathe that first breath of air in a new place. It's always different.*

"I have just come from Sweden, where it was 10 degrees below zero, and the air felt like frozen razors rushing into my lungs, shocking them with the violence of the cold. In London it's a little milder, and my lungs don't protest quite as hard to the cold air. It feels good to be out of the stale aeroplane. I catch the Tube into London and wander around a bit. I only have the day here; I have to hop on a flight again soon. The next time I get off the flight it will be at home.

"I haven't lived at 'home' for over 15 years now, but I still say I'm going 'home' when the flight attendant asks me where I'm headed. I'm going home. It sounds so good to me. Home is walking out of the aeroplane into air so hot and humid that it feels like walking into a wall. All around the tarmac there are palm trees rustling their leaves, singing a song.

"The truth is I say everywhere I'm going is home. I know when I board a plane again in three weeks I'll tell whoever I'm sitting next to that I'm going 'home' to the U.S. too. And when I got on the flight in Los Angeles to Sweden, I told the nice Indian gentleman in the seat next to mine that I was on my way 'home'.

"As I sit in the taxi, which is taking me to my favourite hotel in the world in Colombo, I wonder about this word 'home'. Where

is 'home'? What is 'home'? We're all dashing around from place to place, looking for home. All those clichés come creeping out of the suitcases in my mind: "Home is where the heart is." "A house is made of bricks and stone, and home is made of love alone." The truth is that home is something I carry with me now. After years of rushing around, of travelling, of seeking, I know that home is not a place anymore. Home is those friends I will see. Home is a coconut on the sandy beaches of Mount Lavinia. Home is a hot chocolate on the ski slopes in Sweden. Home is the rodeo in Fort Worth. Home is Joanna, Rebecca, Jake, and Ruby, the friends I will see, the friends I will make.

My parents would sing an old hymn sometimes, "This world is not my home, I'm just a passing through. . . ." I love that line. There is nowhere in this world that will be or can be my home forever. I'm just passing through, and so I have a thousand homes with a thousand people and thousand more I have yet to discover. As the porter opens the car door at the hotel, he recognizes me and grins. 'Hello miss. You have come home again.' I smile back at him. 'Yes Ranjit, I have come home.'

Chapter Six

Tears and Grief

"With one plane ride a TCKs whole world can die. TCKs don't lose one thing at a time; they lose everything, but there's no funeral." [1]

One thing that has greatly delayed the completion of this book is the fact that I wanted to bring a solution to TCKs struggling to embrace, forgive, let go of the negative aspects of their upbringings and, in particular, unresolved grief. I waited for great solutions to appear from the clouds, but have subsequently realised that there is no one universal formula. We are all so different, our experiences so varied, that one person's solution would be another's curse. All I can do is tell you about my own path to healing, and it is still a work in progress.

When I was eleven years old, we were living in India, when word reached us from London that the church storing all of our earthly belongings had taken them to the skip (thrown them away)! The roof had begun to sag under the weight, they had made feeble attempts to get word to us in India to move our things, but what could we do about it from India anyway? The letter didn't arrive in time, so they destroyed all our possessions within the blink of an eye: Furniture, clothing, childhood keepsakes, birth certificates, photos…all gone. This saddened and angered me greatly at the time, since I didn't have many sentimental things to hold on to in life, no childhood teddy bears or baby clothes. Our highly transient lifestyle didn't allow for such luxuries, but now all our remaining possessions had vanished. After our year in India, we returned to England with the contents of our suitcases, still carrying the scent of India, and nothing else. Through the kindness and charity of our Asian friends, most of the furniture was replaced, but a sentimental hole remained.

As I've manoeuvred through my twenties, the discovery of unresolved anger has sprung to the surface. It doesn't seem in fitting with my 'laid-back and calm disposition', but it is very real. With such a rich and exciting upbringing, what could I have to be angry about? Anger at possessions lost; anger at having a mentally handicapped brother; anger of leaving friends, houses, cats behind; anger of not having a place to call home, a place to store my things instead of scattering them across the globe; anger that I only get to see my friends once every couple of years; anger that I wasn't allowed to rebel like other teenagers; anger at having no choice in any of the moves we made; anger that my life is now ruined for the ordinary.

Many of my TCK friends share these angry sentiments and, although they don't jeopardise my daily life, I see how the anger and resentment could fester and eat away from the inside. My anger isn't focused towards my parents or God or the church...these are simply a part of life...but I have found it very healthy to be open and honest, get these frustrations out of my system and put them to bed. My brother and I have had many conversations about these topics and have found a creative outlet for our frustration in things like football (soccer). For me, nothing releases frustration better than screaming at the television during a game along with friends. It is a healthy and necessary release. Without feeling a strong enough affinity with any one nation, Arsenal football club is the equivalent of my national team. Although TCKs face a lot of physical loss in possessions, houses, pets, and friends, it is the emotional aspects that are the most challenging to process.

Throughout my teenage years, I didn't cry much.

I could probably count on one hand the times, and they had nothing to do with transitions or farewells. I had developed a foolproof method of suppression and clothed myself in an excitement for the next destination. When emotions threatened to bubble to the surface during a "farewell", I would simply push them back down where they belonged. This certainly wasn't a conscious decision on my part; I suspect it was simply my coping mechanism for constantly leaving friends, family, houses, and cats. I was very controlled (numb) during farewells, preferring to get them out of the way fast. The hardest farewells for me were with my family members, Samuel in particular, but even then, I managed to push my feelings down. I remember times of sadness when I would try to make the tears come, but they remained in a safe that even I didn't have the combination for.

> *"Unresolved grief is a very real problem for most TCKs, sometimes for the very fact that they have had such rich, adventurous lives. They experience a great number of losses throughout their lives, and James Gould in his review of van Reken and Pollock's book on TCKs, outlines the main areas of loss. The first is 'loss of a world,' because every place, friend and activity that the child once enjoyed is at some point taken away from them, due to their*

*high mobility lifestyle. The second is similar—
'loss of lifestyle,' where all the patterns of
'normal' daily life are stripped away. There is,
of course, 'loss of possessions' along the way,
and one of the most impacting experiences is
that of 'loss of relationships.' A very drastic,
or even abrupt, move can also cause in a TCK
'loss of identity;' for example, as a TCK returns
to their passport country and realizes that it is
not their home country anymore, that they are
not like everyone else. Finally, there is a 'loss
of the past,' for they must give up the past they
knew and also grieve the past they missed out
on by moving in the first place."* [2]

It was only when I got my hands on *Third Culture
Kids: Growing Up Among Worlds* by David Pollock
and Ruth E. Van Reken when I was twenty-one that
I heard for the first time this phenomena of "unresolved grief". In the book, someone suggested it was
helpful to return to the places of your childhood and
say goodbye to the houses and neighbourhoods that
you left behind. This, naturally, was out of the question for me, but I, instead, started pondering all the
moves, houses, and countries I'd lived in, making
lists. I talked it over with my brother and father and
remember feeling anger at not having somewhere to
call "home" and keep all my stuff. I felt a deep sense

of loss and made a conscious decision to explore the grief that lay within me.

I cannot name the place, date, or time, but it was a gradual process, and my heart began to soften little by little. The many farewells of my life came and went, but I hardly shed a tear. I did, however, try to take time to process the events more carefully, writing my feelings down, rather than focusing on the next thing immediately.

My parents paid for my brother and me to go to a counselling place in Switzerland for a week, since we were both at a stage where we had far too many questions and not enough answers. The actual sessions weren't particularly helpful, but it was liberating to just talk about my upbringing…blurt everything out: the good, the bad, and the difficult. No one really gives you that opportunity in life, to really be heard, and (with free license) to discuss your parents in whichever light you chose. Not that I had bad parents but I'd always been very conscious of protecting their reputations through my actions.

Ironically enough, the greatest and most beneficial aspect of that week was reuniting with a childhood TCK whom we hadn't seen in years. We gained far more help from talking to him and the deeper sense of understanding that occurs between TCKs. That, I have come to realise, is the greatest therapy of all. Very few words need to be spoken for a deep undercurrent of understanding to take place between TCKs.

The tears began to fall somewhere along the line, but it wasn't that they were new; it was that I stopped suppressing them. I allowed them to flow when leaving dear faces and places, but it is still an aspect that I am slightly embarrassed about. Maybe that embarrassment comes from the Indian "keeping face" mentality that I was raised in. Sometimes the tears spring from such a deep place that I know I am also weeping for the many losses of the past.

Allowing my emotional side to equal the mental maturity gained through a life of hard and varied experiences has not been easy. It was something I wasn't even aware of until I entered a committed relationship.

Spending time with Indian ladies in Derby, UK, 1981

The Sand siblings: Ben, myself and Samuel, Derby, UK, 1984

Our Sunday School at my parents Asian church, Derby, UK, 1984

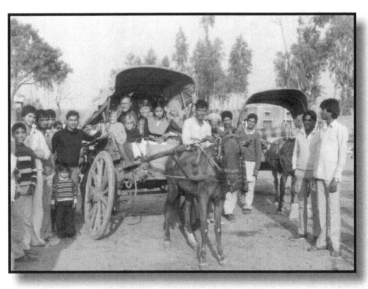

Travelling in style in India, 1986

Encountering different cultures, Jammu and Kashmir, India, 1986

Competing in Sports Day at Hebron School, India, 1987

Punjab, India, 1986

With Ben on our first day at Hebron School. Taken at Montauban Guest House, India, 1987

Front-stage at a crusade in Chennai, India, 1989

With Ben pretending to sell lungis (sarongs) Indian-style,
Kanyakumari, 1989

With Ben watching the Kerala fishermen asses their catch,
Kovalam Beach, India, 1989

A family trip to the Taj Mahal, India, 1991

Coconuts fresh off the tree, Kerala, India, 1991

Taking in the beautiful Norwegian scenery, 1994

Homework time at Montauban Guest House, India, 1995

With my orphanage sisters, Ooty, India, 1998

My adopted English grandmother, Laura Waite,
visiting in Norway, 1996

My mother and adopted Indian grandfather, Frank Stephens,
Nilgiri Hills, 1998

With Paul, newly engaged in Finland, 2007

Our wedding, Kovalam beach, India, 2008

Volunteering at Agape Home orphanage in Chiang Mai, Thailand, 2008/2009

Spending time with Samuel in Dovedale, UK, 2009

Chapter Seven

Education vs. Calling
(social pressures of the Western world)

*When I was growing up, adults always asked
me what I was going to be, but there came a
time when what I was going to be wasn't as
important as who I was.* [1]

Whether studying the American curriculum in
Pakistan, only to return to Norway, or taking a
British-Indian syllabus to England, many TCKs like
myself seem to fall through the educational cracks.
We quite often return home with unrecognised
education diplomas. We become "unfileable". Sup-
plemental courses must be taken, just to meet the
differing syllabus. I myself have fallen victim to this
very thing. My family left India just as I was to enter

the final two years of British schooling (GCSEs). I attempted to continue my education in England but found the curriculum so different to what I'd studied in India that I was at a complete loss. Things were racing on. I was to choose my GCSEs without a proper understanding of the topics and opted for home-schooling instead, since we were moving to Norway. It was a wise decision on most parts, but the home-schooling system was American and entirely different to anything I'd done. Still, I ploughed through my final two years with speed and ease. Unfortunately, the home-schooling association somehow lost my final results, issued a certificate that makes no sense to the average Brit, and, even to this day, I don't know what to fill on forms when it requires my GCSEs. Luckily, traditional further education hasn't been my chosen route thus far, as I decided to do further philanthropic studies with a missions organisation (Youth With A Mission) instead.

In a society consumed with education and diplomas, I do feel inferior at times, even though I believe the best form of education is gained through experience. But I still fear that my educational "mess up" will come back to haunt me one day.

My world geography is pretty good, but when it comes to regional British, Finnish or Norwegian, it's pretty abysmal. My knowledge of world history is as fragmented as my education. It began with basic British/European history, then had parts of advanced Indian and American. Therefore I know a little about a lot of countries, a bit like foreign languages, but big gaps remain. I have an Indian driver's license (which is useless in 90% of the Western world), but I lived in three different countries during the years that most people take their driving lessons and test. It's another thing I just never got around to, due to all the moves.

> *"Real joy comes not from ease or riches or from the praise of men, but from doing something worthwhile."* Pierre Coneille

These are some of my greatest struggles in the Western world, the emphasis on degrees, the drive for material possessions, the way success is measured. There are millions like Mother Teresa, but only one or two are highlighted for their sacrifice. I have no longing or desire to be measured by the hours I've sat in a classroom or behind a desk, but rather the weeks, months, and years spent with the orphans of this world, the downcast, despairing, poor, and needy. The desire to help in some small capacity burns within me so strongly. I cannot rest until the scales of my life tip far greater on that side. So far, I am on course.

Practically and financially, it is extremely difficult to fund these sorts of trips, and having seasons of work appears to be a reasonable option. In this financial climate, it is becoming far more difficult to "raise a support base" like the traditional missionaries did. There are too many leaflets arriving through our doors on a daily basis, asking for help or financial assistance. The other difficult aspect for missionary kids is that their broader friendship network has already been "targeted" by their parents, leaving them with far fewer support options than others.

There are no rules though, and I myself have defied the odds on many occasions and left only with my flight ticket and a bit of spending money. Never have I gone hungry; never have I gone without, and I have done a lot. I am awed to think of how many thousands of dollars I have received for the various missions trips I have done.

I struggle to know where and how I fit into Western society. I have never written a CV (resume), I have done a vast array of jobs, yet never attended a formal job interview, and those things scare me more than moving to a new continent. But more than anything, I have the hardest time finding a work environment that I feel comfortable in and a sense of belonging. I have only worked in an office setting for nonprofit organisations and feel uncomfortable with the unfamiliar aspects of the corporate world.

Many TCKs I know study various things (without ever completing a degree), live in different countries, take random jobs, mostly without long-term commitment or a clear goal. "I can't lock myself into something in case a better opportunity comes up elsewhere; I have to be available to take it." I am guilty of this myself, but it is mainly because I haven't found anything worth studying 4 to 7 years for or a job satisfying enough to lure me in. I guess our fear of commitment in the education or work realms can backfire, since we are happier to float along year after year without realising that life does, in fact, pass you by. It leaves you by the wayside, while the more ambitious climb up the ladders to "success". We may have nothing to show for our antics except memories and photographs, but sometimes that is enough to satisfy our ambitions.

Some missionary kids flat-out reject their upbringing and go down the traditional path (university-degree-partner-house-car-kids); others float meaninglessly, trying to process, forget, or understand what they've been through, and there are those who return to the fold, the safety net of a missions family. None of these are negative, and there are, of course, far more alternatives, but from my experience, these are the most common.

In the missions "bubble", I have found recognition for my qualities, an appraisal for my life experiences, a validation of my upbringing that I would struggle to find in the traditional workplace. And this makes sense because it is what I know the best; it is what my parents did for professions and where I fit.

"Travel is fatal to prejudice, bigotry, and narrow-mindedness, and many of our people need it solely on these accounts. Broad, wholesome, charitable views of men and things cannot be acquired by vegetating in one corner of the earth all one's lifetime." — Mark Twain

Travel opens, challenges, and broadens mind-sets, and in that respect, we are rich individuals indeed. I have gained an appreciation for other countries: their cultures, people, customs...what makes them unique. I don't think you can be too open-minded and respectful of other cultures and people. There is a lot to be learned. The sense of discovery and excitement that can be gained from travelling is amazing, but there is a fine line between escapism and enjoyment.

I think it is characteristic of my generation that we have a harder time putting our finger on our life profession. It seems that some of us have an incapability to decide what to do with our lives. The options are great, sometimes so great that you get swallowed up in them. We float; we wander in search of experience and meaning to this life.

Chapter Eight

Re-entry
(transitions gone wrong)

"I am in that familiar waiting room yet again. Where your departure is too near to fully embrace the country you're in. Your thoughts and emotions have checked out, your tolerance has run dry. You are neither here nor there... , not content in your present circumstances yet unable to grasp what awaits you for it seems too distant and unknown. I feel neither a sadness to leave or an excitement to arrive. Simply confined in the time capsule that has become my life."

— The Waiting Room (of life), HSH, 2007

England to India, 1993

Although most of my many transitions went
smoothly (I somehow managed to remain hope-
ful and excited throughout the farewells, changes,
and new beginnings), some were not quite so easy.
Apart from the natural "first day at school" jitters
and initial hardships of being the new girl, two of
our moves in particular were very difficult for me:

In 1991, we were happily living in East London
and had good friends and a good life. Our world
came crashing down when my parents called us
into their bedroom and told us that we would be
exchanging our London life for a new city in India.
Ben and I tried to change their minds and put up
a good fight, until the night before our departure,
when the familiar butterflies and excitement of flying returned.

The journey didn't go as smoothly as anticipated.
We had an overnight stopover in Colombo (Sri
Lanka) and stayed in a beautiful hotel that boasted
the largest swimming pool in Asia. Early the next
morning, we checked-in at the airport for our Madras flight, but my father soon discovered (with a
sickening feeling) that my mum's passport was missing! He rushed back to the check-in desk, since that
was the last place he'd seen it, and asked the staff to
check behind the desk. They searched but came up
with nothing and advised my mother to contact the

Finnish embassy immediately to get a replacement passport. A tough decision awaited my parents, and the only real option was for us to continue on to India without my mother. My dad had a crusade lined up, starting the next day, and we didn't have the money to all stay in Sri Lanka and wait for mum's new passport. So with extremely heavy hearts, we boarded the plane with my dad, leaving my mum alone in the Colombo night.

My father left us in Madras to attend his seminar. Ben and I stayed with a large family we'd only just met, who gave us disapproving looks when we watched *Baywatch* and *The Fresh Prince of Bel-Air*. Knowing we would be without television in India, we prerecorded our favourite shows and music videos and took them with us to watch over and over again. Those were difficult days, feeling uncomfortable, abandoned, and lost in a strange home with cockroaches roaming in the fridge, in a strange city, parentless.

A few days later, news filtered through from Sri Lanka that my mum's passport had indeed been at the check-in desk, but they had "overlooked" it that night, so she joined us a few days later. Ben and I went to the airport to meet her, happy to see her, but very unhappy with our current living situation.

The realisation that, not only had we swapped the familiarity of our comfortable London life, but also the cool, winding, blue hills of Ooty, for a humid, chaotic, unfamiliar Madras (as it was called back then), left us sad and unimpressed. I retreated to our shared family bedroom, spending most of my time writing letters to friends left behind and friends out of reach (in Ooty).

Upon seeing the only realistic schooling alternative available to us in Madras ("home-school" students crammed into a scorching hot attic space with no ventilation or windows), our groans and grumbles became a little louder. The Nilgiri Hills seemed like the promised land to us, and eventually my parents came around. A phone call to Hebron School was made. They were willing to accommodate Ben and me (even though the term had already begun), and off we went on the Nilgiri Express train to return to the hills of our childhood. What followed were some of the happiest years for my family in India collectively.

I've had more years of education at Hebron School than anywhere else in the world, despite it being fragmented with our comings and goings. I progressed from junior, through middle, right up to senior school levels and know every inch of that school intimately.

India to England to Norway 1995-1996
(the solitary years)

"Your life, my friend, is an island separated from all other islands and continents...you

*yourself are an island separated by its own
pains, secluded in its happiness and far away
in its compassion and hidden in its secrets and
mysteries."*
— Spirits Rebellious by Kahlil Gibran

The second rough transition was when we left
a very happy period in India to return back to the
U.K. Ben had graduated from school, I was fourteen years old at the time and about to move into
GCSEs. I guess it's no surprise that this would be a
turbulent transition, given our age and happiness
with Indian life. We moved to Slough (another new
place), England, in order for my parents to work
with an Asian church there. We stayed with friends
initially, while house hunting, which is never easy.
However, it wasn't I that suffered the most, despite
many failed school attempts, but my mother. She
had a burnout, which is quite normal for returning
missionaries. I can't really tell you medically what
it entails, but I can tell you how it affected my life
as a sixteen-year-old. My mum really struggled with
the transition from her beloved India into a rather
dismal industrial part of the U.K. She didn't leave
her bedroom much and lost all interest in life, food,
and shopping (very uncharacteristic for her). The
weight dropped off. Ben had also taken to shutting
himself away in his room, due to a tumultuous college transition, so it was quite a difficult time.

I embarked upon the hardest schooling transition of my life. In the span of ten days, I started three new schools! The first was far too easy and entirely chaotic. The teachers had long lost their battle for respect with the students, and what ensued was complete disorder and chaos. I came home feeling entirely disconnected from the student body (despite making a friend or two) and couldn't face the thought of returning.

Since the first school was too easy for me, my dad took me to the local grammar school in order to sit an entry exam. I passed, and my mother managed to rise from her bed to take me into town and change my school uniform. This time being the "new girl" was far more daunting, since Slough Grammar School had nine hundred pupils, and I was used to two hundred max. Again I bonded quickly with a few students but struggled to make sense of the curriculum. Hebron, it seemed, ran an entirely different syllabus, and since I was moving into GCSEs (my final two years of schooling, where I was to chose certain subjects to specialise in), they simply didn't match. I came home unhappy, but my parents encouraged me to stick at it a little longer.

I lasted three days in total, but couldn't shake off the restless and unhappy feeling inside. I didn't want to be a burden, since this was a hard time for my family, but I was experiencing inner turmoil. My parents took notice, since this was unusual for me; I usually fit into new schools easily and had certainly mastered it many times before. I begged them to let me home-school (something Ben and I had done briefly in the past), but they convinced me to try one more school.

What would become the final attempt was a local Catholic school at the end of our street. You can imagine what a hassle it had been for my dad simply to get me late admittance into all these different schools. I headed off for my third new school of the week, with a heavy heart and another brand new uniform on. Although I was used to changing schools, the first day, with its butterflies and nerves (feeling out of place), was certainly not something I enjoyed. I gave St. Joseph's School a good go and evoked a flurry of interest from my fellow students. They offered to find me a boyfriend, and take me out on the town, but I felt very, very uneasy inside. I was puzzled by my own inability to fit into any of the schools, and the only thought that brought me peace of mind was home-schooling. I returned home, close to tears, but with more confidence that home-schooling was the right option. My parents came around, and soon enough, I was studying from home. I felt such relief, and didn't even mind about the lack of social interaction.

I don't know what kept me going through that season, but I was happy and content to be back in England. I made friends with a single mother and her eleven-year-old son and spent the weekends at their apartment, watching movies and eating curry. Since I didn't have any friends my own age, written communication with friends around the world took on a huge importance to me.

Laura came down on weekend visits, but even she couldn't entice a laugh out of my mum. *Dumb and Dumber* and *Pride and Prejudice* were the only things that cheered her up during those days. I took over the food shopping duties with my dad, looked after the Sunday school kids at church, and plodded along, until the biggest of all waves came crashing down upon my simple existence. My decision to home-school proved incredibly right with another move lurking around the corner.

Contribution from Debbie Ross (Spain-New Zealand)

"Leaving Spain was the hardest thing I ever had to do. I was 16 years old when I left. As I had spent 6 years of my life there, I had a boyfriend, all my friends, my church, and an amazing country that I had to leave behind. I was devastated!

"My parents had decided that it was a good time to move back to New Zealand, as they wanted us kids to finish our schooling in English. It was a hard transition for all of us, but especially for me, because I had to return for my last two years of high school. I was heartbroken and couldn't understand why my parents had done such a terrible thing.

"Looking back on it now I am so glad my parents made the

call to move us back to New Zealand. This is home now, and I love everything about it... , but, at the time, I couldn't see the big picture, Gods plan for our lives.... . All I was worried about was what was happening then.

"In the months leading up to our departure, I spent a lot of the time super mad at my parents. I spent hours crying, trying to pick fights with my parents, and racking my brain for a way to stay in my beloved Spain. At one point, I even thought about running away from home, but knew that that would never work!

"I took off several times and didn't tell my parents where I was going. One particular time, a few days before we were leaving, I went around to a friend's house. We decided to go to another town, an hour away by train (which I had done many times before), to say goodbye to some friends. This would have been fine, if I had told mum and dad, but because I did it behind their back, they were not happy. I arrived back in town at around 10 PM, to find dad and a friend of his waiting for me at the train station. He was mad because I hadn't let them know, and they had spent most of the day trying to find me. In my mind, I hadn't done anything wrong. There were no cell phones back then, so it wasn't like I could have sent them a quick text.

"Anyway, I was grounded and not allowed to attend a farewell party that a few of my friends from school had planned for me. I was furious!! For months afterwards, I hated them for this. I couldn't understand how they had the right to take that away from me.

"The first few months back in New Zealand were tough. It

was summer and, apart from a few family friends, we didn't have many others.... I was bored out of my brain and so sick of my family. As always, though, God came through for me. I went to a camp, met some great friends, and then, in the fall, started high school and became part of a great group of people, who are still my best friends today. I was still mad at my parents for a few months afterwards, but, with time and prayer, God was able to help me forgive them.

"One big bonus about being a Missionary Kid is that you will have some amazing experiences, travel the world, experience some amazing cultures, and make some incredible friends. I have been lucky enough that I have had the chance to go back and visit my friends every 2 to 3 years. My life is now in New Zealand, but I will always have a special place in my heart for my friends in Spain."

Crossing the Rough North Sea

With the dark winter moving in, exhaustion at seeing my mum's frail state had taken its toll on my dad, and my parents desperately needed a break. A house-sitting opportunity opened up for us in Stavanger (Norway) for five months through family friends. My dad was now dangerously close to a burnout himself, and they both needed time in Norway to recover and get their energy levels up. Rather selfishly, I dreaded the move. Norway had been nothing more than a summer holiday destination for me, and I knew I would have trouble settling in there.

Many TCKs have an Achilles heel within their bouquet of countries, and Norway was that for me. It is far more complicated than not liking the specific country or culture, but factors include the age in which you moved there, the particular stage of life you were in at the time, and the circumstances surrounding the move. Yet again, Ben and I had no choice in the matter. (Although Norway was a struggle for me, I am not blaming the nation itself.)

It was a nightmare as we sailed across the rough North Sea in February of 1996, and I couldn't shake the feeling that I would not fit into Norwegian society. This was true, and my first few months in Norway were terrible...despite living in one of the nicest houses I had ever set foot in.

For me though, I couldn't click with the Norwegian youth. They seemed to be into Satanism, smoking, and getting drunk beyond recognition every weekend. It was a weird contrast, since I was quite a "grown-up" fifteen year old and had hardly touched a drop of alcohol. I continued home-schooling, since my Norwegian was too basic to join a local school, and I didn't want to start yet another international school. The Norwegian dialect on the West Coast was so unknown to me that it sounded like a different language. The cat we inherited with the house had kittens, which kept me busy and entertained, but the initial months were cold and lonely.

Despite all the transitions, I pulled through, and

things eventually got rosy, but I cannot convey how hard, lonely, and isolating it was at times. Of course, I had my family around me (although Ben soon escaped to Los Angeles for six months), and that was completely crucial. During that period in Norway, I lost any desire to go out and make new friends. Most of the Norwegian church girls my mum "set me up with" had as much in common with me as a bar of soap. Their upbringings had been safe and limited, and I couldn't find any middle ground. Through an international church, I did make some friends, mainly because they had multicultural backgrounds and spoke English.

It was through this period that I, perhaps, realised just how different my upbringing had made me. In England, multicultural people had always surrounded us, and it was only going into this very small bubble that brought my uniqueness to light. The journey of self-discovery began, and through hanging out with other TCKs, I was able to put a finger on a lot. It was through the educational pressures of Norway that I decided I didn't want to pursue that path and looked into alternatives instead. I wanted hands-on learning, not classroom. I wanted to get out into the world and enjoy its diversity and the knowledge it had to offer. I suppose I also wanted to escape.

For some reason Norway provoked a little rebellion in me. The patriotism drove me to a broader appreciation of the world around me. I didn't particularly make an effort to improve my Norwegian, because I didn't want people to think I was from there. I became more British and proud of it. I suppose my attitude wasn't the best, in certain ways, but I was sixteen at the time and didn't feel any connection to Norway, so I guess I wanted the bridge to be burned a little.

The other cultural transition I was faced with, for the first time in my life, was with the Americans at church. Despite being an international church, in culture and world view, it was very American. We'd had the odd American at Hebron School (India), but never before had I been so immersed in their bubble and mindset. Neither of the cultures I was surrounded by gave me a sense of belonging, therefore I found a haven with other TCKs.

TCKs are sometimes perceived as snobs, and I guess, at the time, my TCK friends and I did feel a little superior, compared to our Norwegian counterparts, because of the grip we had on the world. In a society obsessed with qualifications and papers, we had already done what most people never dare to do. Venting with my TCK friends is what kept me sane and helped me though that period in Norway.

Norway to India, 1997

"Oh the India of my childhood... . In the long absence, I have romanticized many aspects... ,

chosen to forget the parts I care not for, and clung to the good in an almost fairy tale-like manner. For as long as I've known India, a love-hate relationship goes with it hand in hand. In one fleeting moment, you fall in love with the people, the smiles, the colorful way of life... , the next, you are cursing the power cuts, corruption, and chaos. It's just how things are. But it makes for a rich experience every way you dare to look at it." HSH, 2006

After just under two years in Norway, it was time for my parents to move back to India again, this time long-term. Ben was back at home, after gallivanting in America and Tanzania, and came out with us for the first few weeks. I had finished my schooling and chose not to do further studies, since I was planning on doing a Discipleship Training School with YWAM as soon as I turned eighteen.

My role in India was to help my parents with secretarial things and also spend lots of time with the orphanage girls. I was happy to get out of Norway, but knew it would be weird to return to Ooty and have no ties to Hebron School. The owners at Montauban Guest House had changed and wouldn't let us stay there long-term anymore, so we stayed at another guest house, while looking for a house. We eventually found a lovely new home, and time passed by quickly. I visited Hebron a few times in the beginning, but felt completely out of place. The new students gave me unwelcoming looks, and most of my friends had moved away. So I settled in for a friendless ten months.

It was during this time, being a little older and away from the safety of Hebron School, that I expanded my opinions of India. I really enjoyed how far my pocket money stretched in Rupees but got extremely frustrated with the frequent power cuts, which usually occurred during my favourite TV shows.

By this time, the Internet had arrived in India, so I had another way to stay in touch with friends. In the past, I had sent off letters and waited three to four weeks to receive a reply. Now, within minutes, I could be in touch with friends all over the world. I took great comfort from email, since I didn't really have any friends my own age in Ooty. I spent a lot of time with my mother, bargaining at local food markets, playing with the girls at the orphanages, and travelling by night-bus to Bangalore once a month. That was our shopping "mecca", and we were even able to see the latest releases at the cinema.

In India, you must adapt quickly to the beggars and poverty. They are constant, everywhere, and without a little hardening of heart, you would be an emotional wreck or very poor. I may have a soft core, but upon arriving in India, my hardened mask goes on, and I have no problem telling beggars to go away. Most are "professional beggars" anyway, and the money doesn't go to feeding the child you see before you. The enormity of India's problems puts most people off, but in order to live in that society, acceptance must be granted.

I began to see India in a fuller light, with corruption and greed in action. While living in Norway, we had started to hear bad reports of the orphanage leaders in Kotagiri. Money swindling was apparently going on, and the girls weren't receiving the care that we desired. Now that my parents were to be based in India long-term, they took the opportunity to move the orphanage from Kotagiri (one hour drive) to Ooty, so that they could keep a watchful eye over it and have more involvement in the running of the home. We found a suitable house in Ooty, sorted out schooling for the girls, and told the leaders the date of the big move. The day rolled around, and we were so excited to have our girls closer to us. My mother went to the new house, in order to clean, make the beds, and prepare things, while I went to Kotagiri with my dad to pick up the nine girls. We arrived, full of optimism, but were surprised to see a crowd of people gathered outside the orphanage. We entered the room and saw Jayakumaran (the leader) sitting triumphantly on a chair, with an important looking man next to him. The girls were surrounded by their relatives and wouldn't come to me when I called them. I struggled to understand what was going on, as angry conversations sprouted off in Tamil, and my father and I were on the receiving end of venomous looks. The truth began to emerge slowly.

When the orphanage leader and his wife realised that their unfaithful exploits had come to light, they had written to all of the girls' relatives (most had at least some distant relative alive, although they were unable to care for them) and told them to collect their girls. They made up lies over the reason we were relocating to Ooty and put fear into the hearts of everyone over the children's wellbeing. Jayakumaran and his wife were bitter to lose their jobs and decided to slander us, instead, to clear their own names. Since we didn't have the language or a translator on our side, we couldn't even get our side across to the girls' relatives. I felt sick to my stomach.

The worst was yet to come. The man sitting to Jayakumaran's right turned out to be a police superintendent, who threatened to report that my parents were missionaries and have us deported. I could not believe the evil I was hearing from this couple we'd known for over ten years. We had supported and done so much for them during that time and even given them a job at my mum's orphanage, only to have them blackmail us in the cold light of day. And they hit us where it hurt the most—our girls. I felt enraged, utterly helpless, and heartbroken all at the same time.

My dad tried to reason with this horrible man, but

the damage had already been construed and done. Poison has been fed into the relatives' ears, and they didn't trust us anymore. The superintendent demanded a cash settlement for their silence, something in the realm of Rs. 50,000 (a highly substantial amount for missionaries). All I could think about was how my mum would react when we returned empty handed, having lost all our girls. There was only one girl without any relatives (Rachel) who came with us to Ooty, and she ended up sharing my room, while we tried to deal with the situation. Her father was an alcoholic, who slept on the streets and used to give her alcohol to get her to sleep at night.

My parents continued to fight with Jayakumaran for the girls, and they visited some of the villages where they had returned, but the damage had been done. They saw Sangheeta (one of my dearest) with a shaved head, doing all the village chores. The only way they could afford to keep the girls at home was to send them to work. *Heartbroken* doesn't even cut it. We had clean beds, clothes, food, toys, and school places waiting for them in Ooty, but lies and corruption denied our girls. We managed to get three of the nine original girls back and filled the remaining places with new orphans, who quickly became part of the family.

I grew to love certain aspects of India far more as an adult than I did as a child. The very Bollywood films, chillies, and horrendously loud night bus journeys that I hated as a child bring a wave of happiness over me now. Nostalgia brings an appreciation for things I took for granted as a child.

Although these particular transitions were extremely difficult at the time, through processing them, I have learnt so many valuable life lessons and can look back upon them in a healthy light.

Chapter Nine

Expectation Breeds Rebellion

There is a famous understanding that preacher and missionary kids are the worst of the lot. With so much pressure and expectation connected to our parents on our young shoulders, it is hardly surprising. Sometimes it is too much for a teenager to carry. I guess what I view as "rebellion" is probably just a normal right for a lot of people who have grown up in a less pressurised environment. Although I avoided the "mad at the world" phase that most teenagers go through, I started to dip my toes in the pond of curiosity in my early teens.

At age eleven, my friend and I would smoke paper (with no tobacco inside) on the streets of London, when most kids were on real cigarettes. The Christian school we attended at the time was very "worldly", and I was on track to be pulled into questionable activity during that time. Luckily we moved to India, and by the letters I received from friends back "home", I was saved from a lot of trouble. A little mischief continued in India, but the fear of disappointing my parents and their missionary community, and tarnishing their reputation in our small town of Ooty prevailed.

By default, we had fallen under the rules of Indian Christianity, which viewed going to the cinema, smoking, drinking alcohol, or any such activity as "sin". Indian women are very modest and conservative in dress, and I had to follow suit. None of that really bothered me, but my natural curiosity and cheekiness got me into a spot or two of bother.

As a thirteen-year-old girl, I used to buy teenage books from the local book shop in Ooty and, on one such occasion, my friend and I were browsing through their Sweet Valley High section. I noticed that the book I wanted to buy had a higher price tag on it than a book I already owned (same thickness, same series), and I was slightly angered by this. We cunningly switched the price stickers, covering each other from view, and took them over to the cashier desk to pay.

As the cashier took a closer look at our books, another man came over and whispered something to him. They started deliberating in Tamil, and we just tried to play it cool. Next thing I knew, they were shouting, threatening to call the police, and branding us as "cheats". This, of course, caused a commotion. My friend burst into tears, saying she didn't want to go to jail, and I tried my best to reason with them, pointing out the price inconsistency between the same books. This got me nowhere, so we asked to make a phone call, and my mother came along to pay the difference and save the day. I learnt a big lesson on cheating in general, but especially in India. They can cheat you all day long, but if you do the same to them, it can turn ugly.

During the same period in India, I was on a weekend school trip to the neighbouring hill-station of Coonoor. We stayed at a guest house surrounded by tea plantations and were allowed one trip into town to buy sweets. I was with a different group of friends at the time and someone brought up the topic of smoking. None of them had tried it before, and we agreed to buy a few cigarettes from a *paan walla* (in India, you can buy single cigarettes from stalls) and sneak into the tea plantations to try it. There were three boys and three girls, and we all felt pretty good about ourselves being so rebellious and brave.

Whilst crouching in the tea plantations, having a few puffs, it started to rain, and a few started to panic about getting caught. We put out our cigarettes and started walking back to the guest house when, out of the blue, a few older Hebron students shouted at us from a distance. Paranoia spread in our camp, and one boy in particular was convinced that we'd been seen. He decided to tell his older sister, back at school on Monday, who took it upon herself to go to the teachers and tell on us. I was pretty furious with the whole situation and even more so when I got pulled into the vice-principal's office and discovered that the other girls had decided to pin all the blame on me, the girl from the big, dangerous city of London. The teacher asked me if I'd smoked before in England, assuming it was my bright idea to lead the students astray. He sent me home and then called my parents, and it was with great humiliation that I faced them. Fortunately for me, as a day scholar (a student who didn't board at school), my parents were able to "punish" me as they saw fit, whereas the other students got grounded for weeks. I didn't particularly feel bad for "breaking school rules", but was more angered that we'd been caught, and it became public knowledge. I was embarrassed in front of my parents, though, since my "good girl" reputation had been shattered. My friends and some of the Montauban parents treated me like an outcast, but it only took a few weeks to blow over. Needless to say, I didn't return to the fickle group of friends who dobbed me in, but rather to the ones who gave me a hard time for smoking!

Although these incidents are extremely innocent by most standards and far worse was happening at Hebron School at the time, they felt really bad to me, because of how it could've reflected on my parents, if word had gotten out. I must add that these pressures were not placed upon me directly by my parents; they had little or no choice in the matter. It was simply the consequence of their career choice.

I believe this is one fact that keeps a lot of TCKs out of trouble during their teenage years and delays it until they have moved out from under their parents' roof. The "rebellion" that does occur happens in secrecy, and we become very good at hiding things. When the association of being "so and so's daughter" or son is gone, that is when we can truly start making decisions for ourselves and face the consequences solely.

Fleeing the Nest
(Delayed Adolescent Rebellion)

"I want freedom for the full expression of my personality." — Mahatma Gandhi

As I have mentioned, it was not until I left home that I was able to really discover who I was (independent of my parents) and cement my own opinions and beliefs. Although the process began when I moved to America at the age of eighteen, I had exchanged one "family environment" for another by joining a missions organisation (YWAM). I felt much older than most of my fellow eighteen-year-old students and was drawn to the staff and older students, as well as fellow MKs. I had new boundaries and rules placed upon me, which I was happy to comply with, but my delayed adolescent rebellion (and TCK discovery) was put on hold for a few more years.

I learnt a lot about myself and others during those three years in North America (I also lived in Vancouver) and was able to see more of the world. I was involved in missions trips to Mexico, Thailand, Jordan, Egypt, Israel, Morocco, Spain, UK, and India, and was challenged and stretched within myself. I accomplished things that I never dreamt I could and developed into a more confident individual. I felt very much at home within the mission bubble, surrounded by people from all over the world, and adapted quickly to new situations and environments. I embraced the strengths from my childhood and didn't question too much. During my initial three years with YWAM, I was quickly elevated into leadership roles and took teams to different countries for two month periods. Because I had this responsibility on my shoulders, I continued being the "good Christian girl" and didn't allow anything to distract me from my goals.

It was many years after I initially left home that I was able to find the freedom to push boundaries, experiment a little, and blow off some steam. Having childhood pressure and then going straight into a demanding work environment, where I had massive responsibilities (and was a "role-model"), took its toll, and I wanted out.

I wanted to be selfish and not live in a goldfish bowl anymore. I was sick of people "challenging" me and "speaking into my life". It seemed to me, at times, that Christianity granted free license for people to stick their noses wherever they liked, regardless of whether the person had given their permission or not.

It was while living in fiercely patriotic North America that my mind was drawn to my TCK differences, and I started to question, ponder, and write about it. The *Third Culture Kid* book by Pollock and Van Reken made its way into my hands. It was at this time that I discovered my need to face, not only my unresolved grief, but also the issue of delayed adolescent rebellion. It was revolutionary to know that it was okay to be feeling the things I was feeling and understand it was the natural consequence of my highly pressured upbringing.

I was able to go backpacking in India and South East Asia for five months with my brother and some friends, and it was the exact tonic I needed. No responsibility, no plans, no acquaintances of my parents, no pressure hanging over my head…we could simply enjoy more of this beautiful world and relax. The journey of self-discovery continued on for a few years, as I dipped in and out of YWAM work.

I believe a lot of anger, resentment, and bitterness comes as a result of having to forfeit our teenage years for our parents' calling. In a way, we are unable to push the boundaries and experiment the same way other kids do. But some things follow into our adult lives.

The natural inclination is to worry about what people think, if they see us with a beer or cigarette in hand and now, as an ATCK, I still struggle to shake this off entirely. It has become such a part of my psyche that I still feel slightly guilty for trying "bad" things. It is one reason that I love big cities and the anonymity they provide. The fear of being seen by one of your parents' church members is virtually nonexistent, and I have found that incredibly healthy.

People often don't allow us the time to go through "delayed adolescent rebellion" and feel it is their duty to chastise, instruct, and intervene in our lives. Whether it be friends of parents, people at church, or simply nosey acquaintances who simply can't leave us be, it actually has the reverse affect and stokes the fires of rebellion even more.

With the introduction of modern technology, the world has become almost too small for me at times. The isolation that we felt while on the mission field is no longer the case, by and large. You can now stream favourite TV shows online, watch premier league football (soccer) in the remotest regions of the planet, and video chat with a friend in the jungles of Borneo, all free of charge. Fast food chains are taking over the world, and mobile phones keep you in reach at any given moment. My, how times have changed!

I have found social networking sites claustrophobic, because nowadays parents, relatives, pastors, and old teachers are on them, and I feel pressured to let them into my world. They can now see, hear, and judge my every thought and emotion. Statements can be misinterpreted, and I have found that people speak far more freely on the "unreal" medium of the Internet than they would face to face. All the battles I have fought to break away from those who don't understand me and find solace in obscurity seem to have come undone.

The positive side of this technology is that there is less importance on where you physically live. You can be tightly connected to and in touch with your loved ones so that it makes the pain of separation easier. There are TCK forums and websites where you can connect with other TCKs and find comfort in the cyberworld.

The expectation from our childhood is hard to shake off, not only internally, but outwardly too. The older I become, the more aspects I discover imprinted upon me from my upbringing. Growing up for many years in India, where foreign girls get plenty of harassment from local men, no matter how well covered up they are, has affected my views on modesty. Men and women in India are kept separate and don't interact, under natural circumstances, so everything becomes intensified. As a teenager, I felt so uncomfortable wearing only a swimming suit at Kovalam Beach that I would often wear a T-shirt on top of it. Hoards of Indian men gather at the shoreline to watch foreign "half-naked" women emerge from the ocean. It doesn't matter your shape, size, or age, all women have bestowed upon them the same amount of attention, but the perversity in those men's eyes makes me uncomfortable, even to this day. Speed forward a few years to London, in the summertime, when the girls wear as little as possible, thriving on the whistles they receive from the passing men. I just don't know where I fit in. I don't think it's right to be embarrassed by our bodies, but I also don't feel comfortable flaunting it. I still struggle to shake off some of these issues, even now.

Alcohol is another topic that divides cultures and faiths, but it is one area where I have been able to form my own opinions, irrespective of my parents. I still fall into the old trap, when I visit my parents, whether they be in India, England, or Finland, and have smuggled the odd drink into their home, disposing of the evidence without any of their church members seeing. I think that is one of the biggest forms of "delayed adolescent rebellion" for TCKs who have grown up in communities with religious beliefs and rules. Having been told (not always by our parents, but by the community) what we can and cannot do, listen to, watch, drink, or wear triggers rebellion in many.

In my quest for independence, I caused quite a stir within the Christian Asian community in London. I was twenty-two at the time and had been on a ten-week trip to the Middle East a few years previously, joining in for the final stages of "The Reconciliation Walk" in Israel. [1] I was visiting some friends for dinner, and, among them, was an Indian pastor, fresh off the boat. I observed, as he barked orders to the women of the house, to serve him (even though he was the guest), and sat there as a king. I went for a drive with the afore-mentioned pastor and my friend.

As we passed a mosque, people were pouring out after evening prayers. The pastor spat out something along the lines of: "They are all going to hell, terrorists!". I bit my tongue in the back seat, thinking of all the wonderful Muslims who had welcomed me into their homes across the Middle East and even to a stranger's wedding in Palestine. He continued to make horrendous generalisations about Muslims, and I could hold back no more. Buoyed by my new-found boldness, and despite knowing that a young woman such as myself has no place to speak within Indian culture (particularly to a respected elder), I decided that he could do with a reality check.

I mentioned how wonderful I'd found the hospitality of the Middle East and how the Crusaders had done exactly the same thing between 1096-1099, slaughtering in the name of Christ. He flat-out denied the Crusades, saying, "What rubbish are you talking? We Christians have never done anything of the sort". I told him to look it up in the encyclopedia, because it was historically proven, but he wouldn't have any of it and cut me down to size. I caused quite a stir, and word eventually reached my parents (despite me being a young, independent adult), but they simply laughed it off. In certain cultures, the actions of the children are never separated from the parents (no matter how old the child is).

For me, it has brought a great sense of freedom, forming my own views and boundaries on these topics, irrespective of whether it will ruffle feathers or not. Maybe that is my form of rebellion, no longer having to please my elders (not in a disrespectful way), but just holding on to my own views and philosophies and living by them. That is a huge journey for many TCKs and can take years. For some, it never ends.

Free Will or Inherited Religion?

It is true that many Missionary Kids are put off their parents' religious beliefs, because it can sometimes feel like it's been shoved down our throats. We suffer at the hands of our parents' decisions, and that leaves us feeling like we had no choice in the matter. Having to sit on the platform, facing thousands of people, with a video crew filming the "perfect missionary children" during four-hour Indian seminars was enough to put most people off, but, surprisingly, it didn't have that affect on me.

These things seemed normal to me, because we didn't know any better. We didn't realise that we'd been given the short stick by having to sit through hundreds of meetings, crusades, camps, and seminars, at the age when most kids would just be playing with their friends. Ben and I chose to make the most of it and befriended other kids wherever we went. I was always relieved when my mother was able to sneak us out of the unbearably long Indian village meetings in any number of foreign languages. We would sleep in strange houses and huts until the meal was served (usually around 11 PM).

I did get burned by the church a few times, especially with people promising that Samuel would get healed on a specific date, and it didn't happen. These promises can have catastrophic consequences on a young mind and add unnecessary confusion, disappointment, and pain.

Contribution from Jonny Nease (Cyprus-USA)

"To wander the earth... is it genetic, or is it instilled into the moldable mind of a young child? As an MK, I've found that I am a twenty-one-year-old man with the understanding of someone seeming to be older, with the ability to wrap my brain

around the world—the people, the smells, the ideas, the way others perceive themselves and me.

"Let me tell you a bit about me: twenty-one years ago my parents joined a certain missions organisation (which they still belong to), and we have lived in Cyprus and America. My folks are in the process of moving to Thailand, but that's another story. I've just counted them, and I have lived in two countries, two U.S. states, fourteen houses, and innumerable guest houses, in my solo travels. I own extremely durable rucksacks and suitcases.

"At the moment, I'm on a GH rooftop in Kuala Lumpur, smoking a clove, listening to mellow music, and trying to make sense of it all. I've often wondered at a human's ability to 'get through it'. You see, my life has given me some things...a love for travel, the ability to pack like some mythical hero, and a deep desire to know God, but that's now. It wasn't always like this....

"I used to hate my parents for 'dragging' me from place to place, like a vagabond. I hated Christians for their hypocrisy, and me and God were not on the best terms, by a long shot. Over the course of the last four years, things have been mended, and, in some ways, still are being mended. Specifics escape me at the moment, but as long as I have the Truth, and me and God are straight, that's what truly matters.

"A rather momentous revelation...when me and God are straight, then life is bearable, not easier, but I have a never-ending source of joy, strength, Truth, hope, and power—all the things that are desired and longed for by the world.

"There was a time when my dad and I never really talked.... There was plenty of yelling though. The 'ideal' son I was not.

You see, I have this unique ability to push the envelope, sometimes ripping it into little tiny bits. Anyway, me and my dad both looked at each other as our own personal 'nemesis'. BUT God has redeemed our relationship and, because of that, I know God can do anything.

"As an MK, I looked to my own resilience to make it through all of the moving, leaving, making new friends, and sucked it up when times got rough. But the true strength of a man of God doesn't come from external perceptions; it comes from an unfathomable depth of speaking, back and forth relationship with Christ.

"I know that this is all quite scattered, but what I want to end with is this: We cannot look to our own past. Glean from it all the good you can, but essentially look to the One who created you. All the stories, friends, moving, new passports, and shiftings of heart and mind can be used as a compass to God. Let all the pain go to God, and let it be replaced with His adventure for your life."

I personally was spared from forming a negative association between the duties of my parents' faith and my own beliefs. Many fell away at the wayside, with the pressures and expectations too great, but the only way I can describe it is that God was far too real and present in my upbringing to bother questioning or denying His existence. The sacrifice and selflessness of my parents and their desire to help people, both spiritually and physically, has left a big mark on me, and I strive to live with the same pure intentions as they had and continue to have.

One of the most liberating things about becoming an Adult Third Culture Kid (ATCK) for me has simply been having the choice to decide whether to go to church or not. As a child, often my heart and mind wasn't in church. Because I'd heard and seen it all before too many times, it became a chore and duty to my parents, not a friendship with God. I was put off church for a long while, because I had been overfed it. I had a confused relationship to it. Church was seen as the source of money, and we entered it with a heavy sense of duty to make a good impression on the congregations.

Because of the constant moves, church wasn't a long-term investment; it just spelt the end of more friendships. I still find it very exhausting to this day and see it as new people to get to know (for how long, this time, so is it really worth it)? I've always felt more comfortable in smaller settings, where I have the opportunity to question and understand things for myself (not just quietly accept things), and that is what I have found in London.

Chapter Ten

Friends and Relations
(relating to the world)

"TCKs are not rootless, they are rooted in a different way—through people." [1]

To be honest, this is the chapter I have procrastinated over the most and found the hardest to pen. The topic of friendships is probably what has caused the most pain and frustration over the years and left me feeling deprived. The most important aspect in life is relationships, and my friends have been ripped away from me at every turn. It takes so much energy and effort to maintain hope in new friendships. when you keep losing them all the time.

My appetite for meeting new people is low at the best of times, and I find small talk utterly exhausting. It's a real struggle, because, as much as I long for deep friendships wherever I live, quite often I don't put in the required effort, because I know another move will come along soon enough. This upbringing has given me a good handle on how fleeting life can be and how important it is to make the most of moments with friends and family, but with that comes a cynicism too.

Sometimes I don't see the potential of making a new friend; I see the work involved in getting to know them and quickly analyse whether it's worth it or not. This has been ingrained into my mentality from the routine of making and breaking friends so frequently. I am aware that it is a gamble, since you can miss out on a lot of friendships, but you'd be surprised how attune my powers of observation are and how emotionally draining the process can be for me.

To me, "home" has never been a place, but rather the people who have shaped my childhood. Therefore it is challenging to remain content in one place for a longer period of time, because my "home" is scattered all over the world. I have grown used to the adrenalin that flows with packing up one country in exchange for another, leaving one set of friends for new ones, and leaving one routine for the excitement of the unknown. Of course, it can sound glamorous to some, but there are many hardships that come with such a transient lifestyle. I have gained richness from varied friendships, seeing the world, and knowing people from different cultures and parts of the globe. I have learnt how to relate differently, depending on the cultural or religious background of a person, and that is a true quality. But there have been (and continue to be) many times when I've longed to have a true, close friend in the same room as me, someone who understands me for what I am. Written communication does wonders, but there is no substitute for the bond that occurs between dear friends in the flesh.

I have missed out on a lot. I've had good, close friends for different seasons of my life, but never for longer than a couple of years consecutively. And therein lies the danger of losing touch, the distance coming between you, and the friendship fizzling out. Sometimes you chose different paths, and a few years later, you realise the things you had in common have dissipated. In a way, we have been gifted with the option to discontinue friendships that have hit a dead-end, because of the distance involved.

I have often been surrounded by people who don't fully understand me. In order for people to understand the many facets and undercurrents of my TCK traits, it takes time, and usually time is not on my side. Therefore I have often been mis-understood, and felt alone in a crowd and isolated. Just as you're allowing some of the walls to fall and getting closer to someone, it's time to move on. You begin to hold onto people and circumstances less and harden yourself a little in relationships. It has been a challenge to find the balance between not pushing people away, yet also not letting them get too close. I think the pain attached to losing friends and parting "farewells" will stay with me for many years to come, but it doesn't have to be a bad thing. It's okay to feel pain sometimes, to allow ourselves to admit that we've been robbed. What isn't healthy is when we get caught in a spiral of self-pity and shut off entirely. After all, goodbyes are merely "see-you-laters".

I am not looking for sympathy here. I have many friends around the world, and when I click with someone, it doesn't take long to establish a deep and lasting friendship. The good thing about all of this is that without friends and distractions throughout different periods of my teenage life, I came to an understanding of who I was a lot sooner than most people.

> *"TCKs may have difficulty in maintaining commitments and may avoid solving problems up front (as they have learnt that problems tend to move away)."* [2]

There is a danger with TCKs, to leave conflicts unresolved with people, because we know another move is just around the corner. When things get tough, just pack up and move somewhere else. It is the easy way out, but for non-confrontational people such as myself, a very tempting option. The ability to resolve things in a healthy light eluded me for many years, until I learnt that things catch up to you in life. Sometimes moving seems far more tempting than staying and sticking it out, working it through. But the ability to resolve issues and leave a place well is crucial despite the frequent movings of our childhood.

TCKs

> *"Global nomads recognize each other. Regardless of passport held, countries lived in, sponsoring agency differences, or age, nomads have a sudden recognition of kinship, a sense of homecoming that underlines the powerful bond of shared culture. TCKs also have certain personal characteristics in common. Growing up in the third culture rewards certain behaviours and personality traits in different ways than growing up in a single culture does, which results in common characteristics."* [3]

Just as people who grow up in the same place their entire lives have friends from birth, the gift bestowed upon us is that we can feel a sense of belonging with other TCKs, despite only just meeting them. The natural connection that occurs between TCKs should never be underestimated. It can feel as though we've known each other for our entire lives, despite meeting at different stages of development. It is enough to have someone else to feel out of place with: the company so comfortable, the connection so natural, the conversation so deep, common understanding so true, past experiences so similar, the communion so rich. That is the best therapy known to TCKs. The fact that our upbringings occurred on opposite sides of the globe is irrelevant, because the similarities of our experiences, of being ripped away from homeland after homeland and the heartache and riches it brings, bonds us together in an indescribable way. Some friendships just pick up where you left off, and for me, those are usually with other TCKs, because the understanding goes to the core. The few that I've been able to cultivate and keep (despite the distance) are worth gold. They are worth fighting for.

However there is no point glossing over the fact that sometimes our TCK reunions can be slightly damaging. We delve into life in all its unfairness, our vagabond tendencies, how "home" is a treasure never found, how life is one long transition with hardly any constants, how you spend most your life missing people, wishing you were some place else. Depression can settle in and linger, a negativity towards your surroundings. Spending time discussing these tough aspects of the life of a TCK is helpful, knowing others are experiencing the same complexities but at the end of the day, it doesn't help us embrace our present surroundings.

Contribution from Ann Sung-an Lee (Taiwan-USA-Japan)

"To begin with, my background: I'm born American, to a pair of Taiwanese immigrants, ethnically pure Hakka to be exact, and the first of my family to be born outside Taiwan. At age seven, my parents, who were already travelling ministers, believed God wanted them to move to Japan as missionaries. I grew up in Tokyo and Yokohama, attending international schools, before being forced back to the States my senior year of high school, when they retired from Southern Baptist Mission.

"Straight after finishing university in the States, I moved to Europe and have been living in various countries ever since. I speak Southern drawl to my American friends, Mandarin Chinese to my parents, Japanese for nostalgia purposes, Brit after a few pints, and am regularly immersed in Norwegian.

"The matter of 'where I'm from' has become passé. After around age seventeen, I simply stopped thinking about it. 'Home', for me, has always been where I've made it, a temporary circle of comfort, the company of good friends, the beauty of strange, new places. The paradox of being a TCK: I don't need to be from somewhere; I can be content wherever I am; yet, I never am fully.

"One doesn't have to travel far these days to find fellow travellers, to find people of multiple backgrounds, or to find people who've experienced alienation growing up, whether in the form

of identity crises or some good old fashioned teenage angst. Still, I find it difficult finding that breed of folks who can actually understand how Third Culture Kids think, how it's often not through descriptive words, but unspoken affirmation or acknowledgement. Only TCK's can recognise the struggles in other TCK's proper.

"My parents still bemoan the way I'd been forced to sit still for hours upon end, every Sunday (and sometimes Wednesday evenings) of my young life, preached at in a language I hardly understood. They blame their actions as the direct cause to why today, I'm an atheist, but I hope one day they'll understand it was a more complicated journey then that. Questioning, probing, subverting has been matters of survival. Growing up, it's how I've learned to process new environments and new people.

"One criticism I've heard or one that's often levelled against us TCK's, when we're dissatisfied with a particular place or moment, is either called a 'complaining nature', or an insatiable need to fulfil some 'hole' or 'emptiness' that could otherwise be filled by God, or a mortgage. For one, I really do feel like many underestimate the range of experiences we've had.

"What some interpret as superiority is simply a matter of being able to distinguish what's authentic from imitation. If you've lived in Japan, you know what divine sushi tastes like. If you've gorged on dim sum in Taipei, Chinese fast food in American malls is a joke. If you've been silenced by the Himalayas, Niagara Falls pales in comparison. I also think the desire to travel or the restlessness felt (often aligned with seasons or 4 years) isn't necessarily thinking 'the grass is greener on the other side', but, because the chase for the unknown, in itself, is rich.

"I've been living in a tiny city, Oslo, for some years now, and a few have actually taken offence when I've expressed a desire to leave. 'Why can't you be satisfied with a life here?' 'What's wrong with Oslo?' 'Don't you love your friends, your job?' I say, 'Of course I do,' and my quality of life is very good, but it's static. Domesticity has its merits, of course, and I believe there's a time and place for it, but rest assured, it won't, for me, be done in any typical way.

"But TCK culture is a dying breed because most have been taught to repress their childhood experiences. Of the majority I've known who've migrated back to the States, many automatically assimilate into this 'American deal', or, maybe, what's status quo in the world—go to university, marry, settle down, have babies, plan towards retirement. Filling out a shopping list at Wal-Mart every week, the drone and routines of settled life soon replace the wild, unexplainable memories of youth. My senior year, coming from a utopian-like international school to an all-white, preppie, insular Christian private school pretty much ensured a path towards suicide. Thankfully, I found friends through similar tastes in outside music, art, film, and philosophy. But I've always maintained a scepticism for the expected roles in a Christian setting, in a traditional Chinese family, and obviously in middle class, white America. While some feel perfectly content in security, I think I have always been a freak.

"I think TCK's should be valorised as pioneers of what had, already, back then, been theorised as an increasingly globalised society. We were already well alienated and disoriented before 'postmodernism' hit the books. Now, the power of shared ex-

periences can give confidence to those who feel equipped with
a special knowledge or life experience, but previously didn't
have means to employ it. They are a hidden advantage, when
summoned, worth powerful currency, not some inconvenient
memories, smouldering in the ashes of time."

(Extended) Family

"A unique characteristic of the global-nomad
family is the high degree of interdependence of
family members. Because the nuclear family
is the only consistent social unit through all
moves, family members are psychologically
thrown back on one another in a way that is not
typical in geographically stable families. Close
family bonds are common. Siblings and parents
may become each other's best friends. Patterns
formed overseas fly in the face of conventional
theory about when children leave home, emotionally and physically. ... These 'boomerang
kids' have a need for a strong continuing relationship with parents, the only 'home' they
know. The strength of this family bond works
to the benefit of children when parent-child
communication is good and the overall family
dynamic is healthy. Compared to the geographically stable child, the global-nomad child is
inordinately reliant on the nuclear family for

affirmation, behavior-modeling, support and, above all, a place of safety." [4]

We have always been close as a family, despite my father travelling a lot and Samuel being on the other side of the planet for long durations. For certain periods, my parents became my only friends, and I can see how the lines between parent and child can easily get blurred within the TCK ranks. I think TCK families are more susceptible to parents relying on the children at various hard times (transitions), as the family gets thrown closer together, with the changes and unfamiliarity that surrounds them. It is comforting to have a few constants, when your world gets rocked so frequently. It has meant a lot to me that my family has exercised open communication, and my parents always encouraged us to talk about the difficult times, as well as the good. Now that Ben and I are into our adulthood, it's nice to be able to reminisce with our parents about the many adventures we have shared together.

When living overseas, foreigners tend to congregate together and form their own community. As a result of this, we inherit multiple 'parents' who love to get involved in disciplining us. There are, of course, great aspects of having a global family, people to stay with in every corner of the globe, but it also creates an unnaturally small bubble. Best behaviour must occur at all times, otherwise word will make its way back to the parents. I only had a few encounters with this, and I resented the adults greatly for poking their noses in and attempting to discipline me.

When I was very young, we lived on a Youth With A Mission (YWAM) base in England. We were surrounded by fields, forests, and children from all over the world to play with. One advantage to living in community was always having "uncles" and "aunties" around to help out. I had problems sleeping because of horrible nightmares at the time and couldn't fall asleep without someone staying in the room. There was a young man on the base named Eric, and, night after night, he patiently sat by my bedside, holding my hand until I fell asleep. I'm sure my parents benefited greatly from the broader family gained during those years.

The peculiar currents of my life ended up gifting me with an Indian grandfather and an English grandmother who became far closer to me than my natural grandparents. I see this as a positive, because it wasn't only continents that kept us away from our real grandparents, but also language barriers that stood in the way. I have nothing but fond thoughts, when I think about my grandparents, and a lot of love flowed, but time and language prevented us from forming a close, intimate bond. And it was distance and finance that prevented us from attending any of their funerals when that time came.

Enter Mr. Franklin Stephens of India and Ms. Laura Waite of England, who took up the mantle when we lived in India and England. They showered love, kindness, and hilarious stories upon us and showed us no end of interest. Frank baby-sat us when my parents went on trips around India, and Laura stayed over many weekends when my dad was away (in England).

Laura has the finest laugh in the whole world, to me. She loves to re-tell stories from our childhood, of Samuel's antics, and remembers details better than my parents, at times. I love to hear the stories and laugh endlessly with Laura. She is one of the bravest, strongest women I know, who has overcome many hardships, yet her attitude and positivity is always intact. She has been a dear part of our family for as long as I can remember.

Frank was the legend of Ooty, the most colourful and entertaining character imaginable. He was the most trustworthy Indian we have known, and his stories would go on all day, if given the chance. He remained a very close family friend, until he passed away in 2007, and the sadness I felt was much greater than when my own grandparents passed on. I feel no shame or guilt in saying this, because others stand up to fill the void left by distance and time.

And that is the true beauty of my upbringing. It crossed borders and defied logic, but we lacked for nothing.

Intimacy or the Lack of It

> *"TCKs sometimes appear indecisive and non-committal or have difficulty establishing and maintaining long-term relationships."* [5]

Sometimes TCKs tend to rush things in the beginning, because we know that friendships come and go. Upon meeting new people, we tend to skip the "shallow" levels and get straight to the deep, lasting stuff. For people from different backgrounds, this is quite puzzling, since the natural order of relating appears to have gone out the window. Sometimes our enthusiasm to jump into the "juicy" stuff gets misinterpreted as romantic interest, and can get us in all sorts of trouble.

I learnt that the emotional side of my life wasn't allowed to develop naturally, due to all the disrupted friendships. We delve deep with people for one to two years at the most, then have to start all over again, or choose how far to let the next person in. It's no wonder that we have abnormal gaps between emotional and mental maturity. This can get ironed out over time, but it takes work and commitment from loving people. The many walls and guards we clothe ourselves in need to drop one by one and, for me, that only really started to happen on a complete level when I entered a romantic relationship.

TCK or Non-TCK?

This is a broad and intriguing topic and ultimately, there is no right answer. I began writing this segment many years ago as a single woman, traversing the globe with immense ease, harbouring the desire to find my soulmate.

Almost a decade ago, I was sitting on the porch of my friends' house overlooking a fjord, having a really good conversation with my fellow TCK, David Joseph. We talked about all kinds of things, but one point of conversation that sticks out more than the rest was when we talked about whether it was best for a TCK to end up marrying another TCK, or a "normal" person. We talked through the pros and cons, and it was hard to come to a conclusion as to which we thought would be best. Having another TCK would be great, because you would be able to understand and relate to each other concerning your upbringing, but the danger could be of becoming quite rootless and almost isolated with the people you chose to relate to. With a non-TCK, together you could relate to a broader spectrum of people and learn a lot from each other. I thought it would bring a healthy balance.

Will Anyone Understand the Language of My Soul?

"My heart is worth protecting." I think that best

summed up my attitude towards romantic relationships over the years. I had a few fleeting boyfriends
when I was young, but the older I became, the higher
the guard was up, for the pain of separation hovered
too close. I couldn't see the point of getting seriously
involved with someone who wasn't ultimately des-
tined for me. I thought through the natural order of
events (if it didn't result in marriage) and only saw
the pain I would be left with. Yes, there were people
I liked and people who liked me over the years, but
the minute "the serious conversation" arose, I pan-
icked and backed off. If I couldn't see it resulting in
marriage, I wasn't interested.

I battled internally. In order to follow my heart and
dreams—help the needy of the world—it appeared
that I would end up alone. Life is all about sacrifice,
after all, but I longed for someone to share the experiences with, someone to understand the language of
my soul. But without staying anywhere for longer
than a year or two, how on earth would *he* be able
to get to know me properly?

Life has its own way of answering the big questions, and the man who swept me off my feet was
not a TCK and has possibly had the most polar-
extreme upbringing, to me. He grew up in a suburb
of Auckland, New Zealand, lived in the same house
his entire childhood, and grew up with the same,
steady friends and environment.

He left his homeland in search of adventure and

experience, and that is when our paths crossed. I was living in London at the time, studying counselling, and working with Steiger (a sub-division of YWAM). There was a vacant room in the YWAM house, so my leader invited Paul and his brother to move in. We got to know each other really well that year in London and remained close friends afterwards when I lived in Thailand, Derby, Nottingham and Harpenden for short durations. Paul joined my brother and I on a Christmas trip to India in 2006 and that is when our friendship blossomed into something more.

The light bulb went off in Paul's head when we were visiting Ooty (Montauban of all places), he proposed in Finland nine months later, and we were married at my beloved Kovalam Beach (India), with guests from ten different nations. In our two years of marriage, we have been around the world twice, stayed in over thirteen houses and lived on three continents.

Initially it was a big struggle for me to let my walls down and adapt to communicating and working things through. When faced with confrontation, I would freeze up and want to run. I had grown quite comfortable in my own company and felt suffocated at times. All the emotions that had laid dormant suddenly reared their ugly head, and I had to try to make sense of them, instead of pushing them back down. Adapting to a new country seemed far easier to me than adapting to another person. There is nowhere to hide. The learning curve is great and continues daily. I have cleared most of the trickiest hurdles and have gained a new home in the process.

Despite our extremely varied upbringings, Paul understands my soul better than anyone and has made a huge effort to understand my TCK tendencies. That is where it all lies, having the capacity and desire to understand each other's background and allowing each other the space to be different.

Home

by Paul Matthew Hart

She says she never had a home,
A place to truly call her own.
First here, then there, never anywhere.
Not long enough to establish roots,
To feel at home, to reap the fruits.

Well, I fell in love with her today.
It all feels right, it feels okay.
But here we are, you and me,
Love ... Uncertainty.

If you'll allow
Forever, no loan,
I'll give to you.
I'll be your home.

Call me the patriot,
To colours, black and blue,
To God, NZ, and You.
To toes in sand,
And wrinkly hands,
From swims in oceans blue,

I see it's tough.
I speak of home,
With glowing truth.
But now my truth is
Home is you.

If you'll allow
Forever, no loan,
I'll give to you.
I'll be your home.

February, 2007

Epilogue

During the writing of this book I have been immersed, both in thought and emotion, in all the things that make us TCKs so different from the rest of society. I have often caught myself thinking that no one will be able to understand me since I am so different; my estranged mindsets and beliefs all take root in certain experiences or episodes from the past, and I will never be able to find someone who was present at all of those events.

But I have realized that these are the unimportant things in life. Bonds can occur in a matter of minutes, and new life-long friends await around the unexpected corners of life. The TCK label isn't as important as I once thought it to be. At the end of the day, we are all human beings and can find some common ground, if we try hard enough. Yes, we should cherish our TCK differences, strengths, and knowledge, celebrate them even, but not allow them to become the excuse for keeping others at bay. We posses the ability of uniting different kinds of people and groups of friends, so use it.

For non-TCKs, if you believe it to be an overwhelming task to understand and relate to us, then you are mistaken, because underneath the surface, we are just like everyone else.

If you enjoyed this book, please spread the word:

http://homekeepsmoving.blogspot.com

homekeepsmoving@gmail.com

References

Front Matter:
1. Other than the two lines marked with an asterisks, these quotes are from Andy and Deborah Kerr, *You Know You're an MK When...", 1999.* The lines marked with an asterisks are anonymous.

Chapter One:
1. Pollock, David C. and Ruth E. Van Reken. 1999. *Third Culture Kids: Growing up Among Worlds.* Yarmouth, MA: Intercultural Press, page 19.
2. John Brockman, *The Third Culture: Beyond the Scientific Revolution,* Simon & Schuster: 1995. Taken from Wikipedia.
3. Pollock, David C. and Ruth E. Van Reken. 1999. *Third Culture Kids: Growing up Among Worlds.* Yarmouth, MA: Intercultural Press, page 39.

Chapter Two:
1. An interview with David Pollock (sociologist/TCK expert).
2. Pollock, David C. and Ruth E. Van Reken. 1999. *Third Culture Kids: Growing up among Worlds.* Yarmouth, MA: Intercultural Press, page 81.

Chapter Four:
1. Iwama, 1990.
2. Pollock, David C. and Ruth E. Van Reken. 1999. *Third Culture Kids: Growing up among Worlds.* Yarmouth, MA: Intercultural Press, page 79.

Chapter Five:
1. Cowley, Malcom. 1991. *Exiles Return. In An Assessment of Reentry Issues of the Children of Missionaries,* ed. Doris L. Walters. New York: Vintage Press, 117-118.
2. Anonymous, taken from http://www.thirdculturekid.blogspot.com

3. Brian Lev, as quoted in: Norma M. McCaig, Foreign Service Journal, September 1994, pp. 32-41.

Chapter Six:
1. Pollock, David C. and Ruth E. Van Reken. 1999. *Third Culture Kids: Growing up among Worlds.* Yarmouth, MA: Intercultural Press, page 167.
2. Rall-Heiderich, TCK article, International Studies Seminar, April 29, 2005. ibid, 77-78

Chapter Seven:
1. Anonymous missionary kid

Chapter Nine:
1. The Reconciliation Walk was an interdenominational grassroots movement of Western Christians, retracing the route of the First Crusade, apologizing to Muslims, Jews, and Eastern Christians for the atrocities that accompanied those Crusades.

Chapter Ten:
1. Lorena Smith.
2. K.A Jordan, 1998. "Third Culture Kids: Returning to their Passport Country" by Julie K. Kidd, George Mason University and Linda L. Lankenau, International School of Santo Domingo and former Foreign Service Officer. This article originally appeared in Syllabus, a publication of Phi Delta Kappa, Chapter 1144. 4, 5.
3. Norma M. McCaig, *Foreign Service Journal*, September 1994, pp. 32-41.
4. Norma M. McCaig, *Foreign Service Journal*, September 1994, pp. 32-41.
5. Norma M. McCaig, *Foreign Service Journal*, September 1994, pp. 32-41.